THE PILOT TRAP

The Category Error Behind Enterprise AI Failure

Published by VJ X AI
Melbourne, Australia

First Edition, 2026

A catalogue record for this book is available from the National Library of Australia.

THE PILOT TRAP

The Category Error Behind Enterprise AI Failure

VIJAYAN SEENISAMY

CONTENTS

FOREWORD

The most expensive sentence in enterprise AI is: "The pilot was a success."

I have heard it in boardrooms for twenty years. Large enterprises, government organisations, fast-moving consumer brands, telcos, not-for-profits trying to change the world. Different sectors, different pressures, same pattern. The demonstration is compelling. The business case is funded. The quarterly update signals progress. And somewhere between the steering committee's approval and the system's third month in production, the returns quietly fail to arrive. Nobody can name exactly when. Nobody can name exactly why. The dashboard still shows green.

This book names exactly why.

Vijayan and I arrived at the same structural diagnosis from opposite ends of the enterprise. We were two of four co-authors on the Intelligence-Centred Enterprise research, building a shared argument that AI value is fundamentally a leadership and organisational change problem, not a technology problem. I came at that argument from the strategy layer, testing it with CXOs across industries: that enterprises treating AI as a tool to deploy are losing ground to those treating it as an operating model to build. Vijayan came at it from inside the delivery machine itself, asking a sharper and more uncomfortable question: why do competent teams, using proven methods, consistently fail to sustain AI systems in production?

His answer is the most rigorous structural diagnosis of enterprise AI failure I have read. The argument is deceptively simple. The delivery model that has governed enterprise technology for thirty years was designed for systems that behave the same way after deployment as they did during testing. AI systems do not behave that way. They drift. They degrade. They produce different outputs from the same inputs depending on context, data state, and conditions nobody fully controls. Every management practice downstream of that mismatch, the governance, the roles, the economics, the success metrics, produces results that look correct and are not.

Vijayan calls it the category error. Once you see it, you cannot unsee it. And once you understand it, the conventional explanations for AI failure, data quality, talent gaps, integration complexity, executive sponsorship, stop looking like root causes and start looking like symptoms. That reframing changes the conversation entirely, because it means solving any one symptom in isolation will never solve the problem.

What makes this book dangerous, in the best sense, is that it does not let anyone off the hook. Not the CIO who approved the programme. Not the CFO who funded it. Not the delivery leader who executed it faithfully using methods that were structurally wrong for the task. I have sat in too many steering committees where the quarterly update conflated activity with production. Where the system was technically on track and structurally failing. Where everybody measured what was easy to measure and nobody measured what mattered. If you have sat in those rooms, these twelve chapters will give you the language to name what you already sense is broken.

But Vijayan does something here that separates this book from the growing pile of AI strategy commentary. He builds the replacement, not just the critique. System stewardship as an operating discipline. Five control surfaces that define the minimum viable governance for probabilistic systems. A role architecture for accountability that does not yet exist in most organisational charts. And a five-agent diagnostic you can run this week that will reveal what has been invisible since deployment. This is not a book that diagnoses a burning building and walks away. It hands you the blueprint and tells you where to start.

The timing matters. Enterprises are accelerating their AI investment at the precise moment their delivery models are least equipped to sustain it. Autonomous agents are entering production faster than any framework exists to govern them. Every quarter that passes without addressing the structural cause does not just waste capital. It compounds waste, builds false confidence, and widens the gap between what the organisation believes about its AI capability and what is actually true.

Read this book the way Vijayan wrote it: as a structural argument backed by evidence, designed for the executive who is accountable for AI outcomes and ready to hear why the current approach is not working. It will not make you comfortable. It will make you effective.

Mark Cameron
Mark Cameron is Founder and CEO of Alyve (Human Kind Technology), a Forbes technology strategy columnist, and teaches Digital Transformation Leadership in the Executive MBA programme at Deakin University.

Melbourne, 2026

WHAT THIS BOOK IS

Enterprise AI pilots work. The demos are compelling. The business cases are funded. The technology reaches production, and then it fails in ways the delivery model was never designed to detect.

The cause is structural. The delivery discipline that governs enterprise AI was designed for deterministic systems. AI systems are probabilistic. Every management practice downstream of that mismatch, the governance, the roles, the economics, the success metrics, produces results that look correct and are not. This is not a governance framework or a compliance guide. It is a structural diagnosis and the operating discipline that addresses it.

This book names the root cause, builds the replacement discipline, provides the evidence that the discipline works where it has been practised, and gives you a one-week diagnostic you can run on Monday morning. It is written for the CIO, CAIO, CTO, CFO, or CEO who approved the AI investment and is now asking why the returns have not arrived.

PREFACE

When AI entered the enterprise programmes I was leading, I applied the same delivery methods that had worked for every technology I had ever deployed. I had spent twenty years leading delivery programmes and digital transformations across manufacturing, retail, banking, telecom, insurance, media, and public sector. I had restructured delivery functions, designed operating models, and governed programmes large enough to appear in board papers. The methods were rigorous. They were proven. And they produced the same results that every other enterprise was getting: pilots that impressed and production systems that failed silently. Research from MIT, S&P Global, and Camunda would later confirm the pattern at structural scale. Ninety-five percent of enterprise AI pilots fail to reach reliable production. That is not experimentation. That is systemic capital destruction. The number did not surprise me. By then, I had seen enough to know it was not a talent problem or a technology problem. It was a delivery system problem. And delivery systems do not quietly fail. They compound waste. They create false confidence. They allow quarterly reports to signal progress while production reality erodes.

What I found when I examined that problem was not what I expected. The failure was not in the teams. It was in the methods themselves. The delivery model I trusted was designed for systems that behave the same way after deployment as they do during testing. AI does not behave that way. The model was structurally incompatible with the technology it was governing, and I did not see it until the pattern had repeated enough times to become undeniable. In practice, this looks like the same scene in every enterprise:

a quarterly review where the project team reports success, the system has been silently degrading for weeks, and nobody in the room has the data or the authority to surface the gap. That recognition became the foundation for the AI Role Operating Framework™ (AI ROF™), a model for how enterprises must restructure accountability when the technology is probabilistic, and it identified four leadership roles that the discipline requires: the AI Architect, the AI Product Manager, the AI Delivery Manager, and the AgentOps Lead.

I had planned to write this book first. The structural diagnosis. The explanation for why enterprise AI fails at scale and the operating discipline that addresses the gap. But I kept arriving at the same problem: I was describing a system that required roles no enterprise had defined. I could not explain how the discipline worked without first explaining who would practise it. That detour became *The AI Delivery Manager Blueprint*, published in January 2026, which defined one of the four roles in depth. The response confirmed what the data already showed: the gap is real, it is structural, and it is felt at every level of the enterprise.

But defining one role out of four is not defining a discipline. An enterprise that hires an AI Delivery Manager without building the operating system around them will produce a title change, not a structural correction. The role without the system is accountability without architecture. This book sits above any single role. It diagnoses why enterprise AI fails at structural scale, names the root cause that a thirty-year-old delivery model was never designed to reveal, defines the operating discipline that addresses it, and provides the evidence that the discipline works where it has been practised.

You have heard other explanations for the failure rate. Data quality. Talent shortages. Integration complexity. Executive sponsorship gaps. This book does not dismiss them. It argues they are downstream symptoms of the same structural cause: a delivery system designed for deterministic technology, applied without modification to probabilistic systems. Until that cause is addressed, solving any one symptom in isolation does not solve the problem. Chapter 2 makes the case in full.

This book is written for the CIO, CAIO, CTO, CFO, or CEO who approved the AI investment and is now asking why the returns have not arrived. If you are responsible for AI performance, you are already accountable for a system that was never designed to govern it. It is for the transformation leader who can see something structural is wrong but has not yet been able to name it. And it is for the emerging AI delivery function, whatever it is called in your organisation, that must now build the discipline these pages describe.

The discipline is designed for the hardest case: autonomous agents that make decisions and take actions with minimal human oversight. If the operating discipline works for agents, it cascades to every AI system that behaves probabilistically. A chatbot, a recommendation engine, a document classifier. The structural mismatch is the same. The agents are where the consequences compound fastest.

Three sections. Twelve chapters. The first four diagnose the structural failure. The next four define the discipline: what system stewardship requires, the control surfaces it operates through, the roles it depends on, and the operational philosophy that sustains it. The final four provide the evidence that it works, the convergence of forces that makes it urgent, a self-assessment that tells you where you stand, and a five-agent test you can run this week. It tells you what to build and where to start. The implementation belongs to your teams and the practitioners who will operate the system.

The claim at the centre of this book is large: that the delivery discipline for enterprise AI does not yet exist in most organisations, and that its absence is the structural explanation for a ninety-five percent failure rate that is not improving. The chapters that follow build the evidence for that claim and then build the discipline itself. I would not make the argument if I had not seen both the failure and the correction from the inside.

PART I: Diagnosis

The pilot succeeds because the conditions are artificial. Production fails because the conditions are real.

VIJAYAN SEENISAMY

CHAPTER 1

The Pilot Trap

Every enterprise with a meaningful AI investment is now confronting the same question. Not whether the technology works. It does, demonstrably, in every pilot and proof of concept that reaches the steering committee. The question is why it stops working when it reaches production.

MIT researchers studied 300 public AI deployments, surveyed 350 employees, and interviewed 150 executives across industries. Their finding: 95% of enterprise AI pilots fail to deliver measurable impact on the profit and loss statement. Not 50%. Not 70%. Ninety-five percent.

The precise number is debatable and has been debated. Critics have questioned whether MIT's sample composition conflates organisations that never intended to reach production with those that tried and failed, and whether the methodology behind the headline figure is sufficiently transparent. These are fair criticisms of any single study. What matters more is the convergence across independent institutions. The same conclusion emerges from S&P Global's abandonment tracking, Camunda's production deployment survey, Gartner's cancellation forecasts, and ADAPT's CFO research. Five institutions, five methodologies, five populations, one pattern. The precise number matters less than the convergence. The technology works. The delivery system does not.

That number should stop a board meeting. It rarely does, because most boards never see it. What they see instead is a pipeline of successful demonstrations, a portfolio of promising pilots, and a quarterly update that conflates activity with production. The AI programme is expanding. The team is delivering. The technology is impressive. The returns are not materialising, and the reporting structure is not designed to make that visible until the gap becomes a crisis.

The pattern is consistent across industries, geographies, and company sizes. Enterprises are spending more on AI every year. They are launching more pilots. They are seeing more impressive demonstrations. And they are failing to convert those pilots into production systems that deliver sustained, measurable business value at anything close to the rate their investment requires. Something structural is broken between the pilot that succeeds and the production system that does not. Most enterprises have not yet named what it is.

MIT SLOAN MANAGEMENT REVIEW / S&P GLOBAL,
NANDA Initiative, 2025 (150 executive interviews, 350-employee survey, 300 public AI deployments).

THE PATTERN THAT IS NOT IMPROVING

If the 95% number were an artefact of early adoption, the trend would be improving. It is not.

S&P Global Market Intelligence tracked enterprise AI abandonment rates across 2024 and 2025. In 2024, 17% of companies had abandoned most of their AI initiatives. By 2025, that number had jumped to 42%. The average organisation scrapped 46% of its proofs of concept before reaching production. Abandonment did not halve as the technology matured. It more than doubled.

S&P GLOBAL MARKET INTELLIGENCE,
2025.

Camunda and Coleman Parkes surveyed 1,150 senior IT decision makers across the United States, United Kingdom, France, and Germany in a study published January 2026. Of those deploying AI agents, only 11% had reached full production status. Seventy-one percent of organisations said they were using AI agents. Eleven percent had made them work reliably in production. Seventy-three percent reported a significant gap between their agentic AI vision and their operational reality. The gap between ambition and delivery is not narrowing. It is widening, and it is widening at precisely the moment enterprises are accelerating their investment.

CAMUNDA / COLEMAN PARKES,
2026 State of Agentic Orchestration and Automation (1,150 senior IT leaders, January 2026).

Gartner's projection extends the pattern forward. More than 40% of agentic AI projects will be cancelled by the end of 2027 due to escalating costs, unclear value, or inadequate risk controls. The problem is not decelerating. It is compounding.

GARTNER,
Agentic AI Project Cancellation Forecast, 2025.

Australian enterprise data tells the same story from the CFO's perspective. ADAPT's research across Australian CFOs found that 77% of CFOs say their organisations are not effectively realising value from AI. Only 4% report being "very effective" at generating AI value. The technology is being purchased. The investment is being made. The returns are not materialising, and the CFOs closest to the numbers already know it.

ADAPT,
CFO Edge Research, November 2025.

These are not isolated findings from a single methodology or a single year. Five independent research organisations, studying different populations across different timeframes, converge on the same conclusion. The enterprise AI delivery system is failing at structural scale. The technology is not the common denominator. The delivery system is.

The consistency of the findings matters. MIT studied deployed systems. S&P tracked abandonment trends. Camunda surveyed decision makers at the point of deployment. Gartner projected forward from current trajectories. ADAPT surveyed Australian CFOs at the point of value realisation. Each approached the question from a different angle. Each found the same structural gap. When five independent lenses produce the same diagnosis, the problem is not a sampling artefact. It is a systemic condition, and it requires a systemic response.

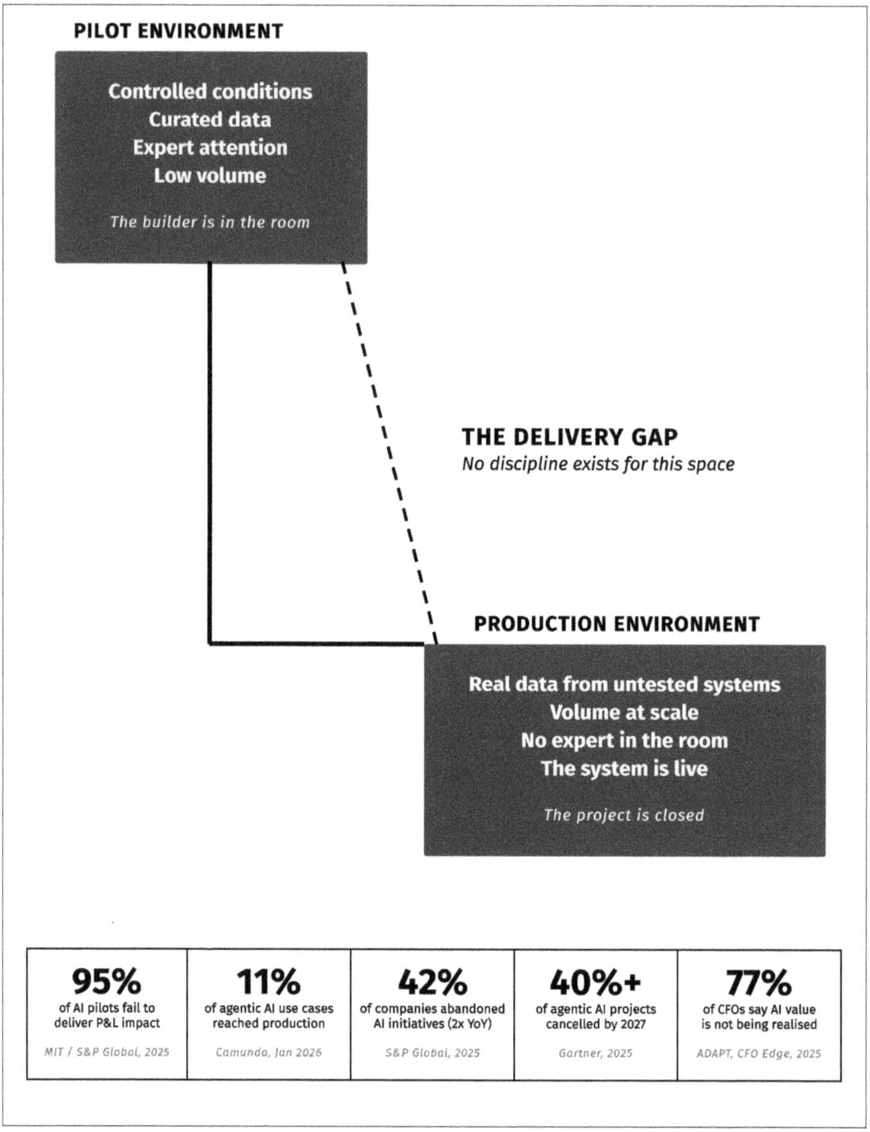

The technology is not the common denominator. The delivery system is. Five independent research organisations, using different methods and populations, found the same structural gap.

FIGURE 1.1
The pilot to production cliff

WHAT THE PILOT OBSCURES

The pilot succeeds because the conditions for success are artificially assembled. A small team of the organisation's best engineers works on a single use case with curated data, direct access to stakeholders, and constant expert attention. The volume is low. The edge cases are few. The environment is controlled. When something goes wrong, the person who built the system is in the room to fix it before anyone notices.

Production is different in every dimension that matters. The data arrives from systems the pilot team never tested against, carrying inconsistencies, missing fields, and edge cases that curated datasets do not contain. Volume scales by orders of magnitude and exposes failure modes that low-volume testing could never surface. A customer-facing agent that handles fifty interactions a day during a pilot handles five thousand in production, and the error rate that was invisible at fifty becomes a reputational crisis at five thousand.

Edge cases multiply because real users do not follow the paths the pilot anticipated. They ask questions the system was not designed for, provide inputs in untested formats, and interact in sequences nobody imagined. Meanwhile, the team that built the system has moved to the next project. The person monitoring performance, if anyone is monitoring it at all, does not know what "normal" looks like for this particular system.

The most dangerous characteristic of the pilot-to-production transition is that it is not a scaling problem. It is an environmental shift. The system moves from a setting optimised for demonstration to a setting defined by variability, and the management framework that governs the system does not change to match. The same project plan, the same success metrics, the same staffing model, the same governance structure that worked in the pilot are applied to a production environment that resembles the pilot in name only.

Consider what changes between pilot and production at the level the management framework does not track. In the pilot, the data was selected by the team that built the system. They knew its structure, its edge cases, its limitations. In production, data arrives from upstream systems the pilot team never tested against, carrying format inconsistencies, missing fields, and encoding artefacts that curated pilot datasets never contained. A prompt that performed reliably against clean data produces unpredictable results against messy data, and the monitoring infrastructure, designed for deterministic systems, sees nothing wrong because the system is technically operational.

In the pilot, cost was a line item in the project budget. Nobody tracked per-task economics because the volume was too low to matter. In production, token consumption scales with every interaction. A customer support agent that processed fifty queries a day during the pilot processes five thousand in production. The inference cost that was invisible at fifty becomes a material budget variance at five thousand, and the finance team has no mechanism to connect the variance to the specific agent that caused it because no cost-per-task metric exists.

In the pilot, governance was informal and embedded in the team. The person who built the system was also the person who caught problems and fixed them before anyone noticed. In production, the build team moves to the next project. The system is handed to an operations team that was not involved in its design, does not understand its calibration, and has no evaluation framework for judging whether its outputs are acceptable. Governance becomes a quarterly review against criteria that were written for a different kind of technology, and between reviews, the system operates without structured oversight.

In the pilot, the definition of success was binary: does the system work? In production, success is a spectrum: is the system still working well enough, and how would you know? The pilot answered the first question. Nobody designed the infrastructure to answer the second.

The project is marked complete. The system is marked live. And the gap between what the dashboard says and what the system actually does begins to widen.

This gap is invisible for weeks or months. The system continues to operate. Outputs continue to be generated. Costs continue to accumulate. But nobody is measuring whether the quality of those outputs is degrading, whether the costs have crossed the threshold where the agent task costs more than the human equivalent it replaced, or whether the system's behaviour has drifted outside the boundaries the governance framework assumed it would stay within. The pilot trap is not that the pilot fails. The pilot trap is that the pilot succeeds, and that success blinds the organisation to everything that happens next.

The pilot's success is the trap. It becomes evidence that the system is ready for production. It is not. It is evidence that the system works under conditions production will never replicate.

THE WRONG DIAGNOSIS

The most common response from enterprise leadership is that this is a maturity problem. New technology, growing pains, early adoption curve. Given time, the argument goes, organisations will learn to deploy AI reliably the way they learned to deploy ERP, cloud, and mobile. The analogy is comforting. It is also wrong.

The S&P data dismantles this directly. If the problem were developmental, abandonment rates would decrease as organisations accumulated experience. They doubled in twelve months. Gartner is projecting accelerating cancellations through 2027, not decreasing ones. Enterprises that have been investing in AI for three or four years are not showing materially better production rates than those that started eighteen months ago. This is not a learning curve. It is a structural mismatch between the delivery system and the technology it is attempting to deliver. More experience with the wrong delivery model does not produce better outcomes. It produces more expensive failures.

The CFO sees this pattern before anyone else, because it shows up in the numbers with uncomfortable clarity. AI spending is growing. Gartner estimates worldwide AI spending will reach $2.5 trillion in 2026, a 44 percent increase year-over-year. Enterprise after enterprise is increasing investment while failing to convert that investment into production systems that generate measurable returns. A CFO looking at a rising cost line and a flat return line is not looking at a maturity problem. They are looking at a capital allocation failure that compounds every quarter it continues. The business case that justified the pilot assumed production-scale returns. Those returns require production-scale reliability. That reliability has not arrived.

MIT and BCG's research on the emerging agentic enterprise confirms the acceleration on the technology side. Thirty-five percent of enterprises are already deploying agentic AI. These are autonomous agents that make decisions and take actions with minimal human oversight. The technology adoption is racing ahead of any framework for managing it. Organisations are deploying agents faster than they are building the capability to govern, evaluate, or operate them reliably. The velocity of adoption is widening the gap, not closing it. Every new agent deployed without the delivery discipline to sustain it adds to the portfolio of systems that will fail silently in production.

A reasonable objection at this point is that the evidence conflates different kinds of AI. A chatbot that answers customer questions is not the same system as an autonomous agent that makes lending decisions. That is true. But the delivery challenge is the same in kind, if not in degree. Every system that uses a large language model is probabilistic. Every system whose outputs vary with context, data state, and model updates requires continuous evaluation that the deterministic delivery model does not provide. The chatbot that "works fine" is a probabilistic system governed by a deterministic delivery model. It has not failed yet. The question is whether anyone in the organisation would know when it starts to.

Agentic systems are where the consequences compound fastest, because agents make decisions, take actions, and operate across multiple steps with minimal human oversight. The agentic case makes the structural mismatch impossible to ignore. But the same mismatch applies to every enterprise AI system that behaves probabilistically. The discipline is designed for the hardest case. It cascades to the simpler ones.

THE INHERITED ASSUMPTION

There is a reason this is happening, and it is not incompetence. For thirty years, enterprise technology delivery has operated on an assumption so reliable that nobody questions it: if you specify the requirements, build to specification, test thoroughly, and deploy carefully, the system will behave in production exactly as it behaved in testing. This assumption is the water the enterprise swims in. It is so foundational that it does not appear in any project methodology as a stated premise. It does not need to. It is the premise that every methodology was built on. This is the thirty-year satisfying assumption: the belief that a system tested is a system finished. It served the enterprise well for every technology that came before AI.

AI systems do not behave this way. They change without warning, degrade without defects, and produce different outputs from the same inputs. The assumption does not hold.

That mismatch between the delivery system and the technology it governs is not a minor gap. It is a category error. The delivery system was designed for one kind of system and is being applied to a fundamentally different kind of system. And it is the structural explanation for why 95% of enterprise AI pilots fail to reach reliable production. Not because the technology is immature. Not because the teams are unskilled. Not because the investment is insufficient.

Because the delivery system they are using was designed for a fundamentally different kind of technology, and the harder they apply it, the wider the gap becomes.

You do not have an AI problem.
You have a thirty-year-old
delivery model applied to
a technology it was never built for.

VIJAYAN SEENISAMY

CHAPTER 2

The Category Error

Every one of these practices produces results that look correct and are not. When you misclassify a system, every management decision downstream inherits the mistake. Your testing methodology, your governance model, your staffing assumptions, your budget architecture, your success metrics: all of them were designed for a kind of system you are no longer operating.

THE THIRTY-YEAR INHERITANCE

For three decades, enterprise technology delivery operated on a reliable assumption: if you define the requirements precisely, build to specification, test thoroughly, and deploy carefully, the system will behave in production exactly as it behaved in testing. This assumption was not wrong. For deterministic software, it was the foundation of every successful delivery methodology ever written.

Waterfall assumed it. Agile refined the cycle time but kept the assumption intact. DevOps automated the deployment pipeline, but the pipeline still moved a deterministic artefact from one environment to another. Even site reliability engineering, which introduced the idea of production operations as a discipline, was designed for systems whose failure modes are visible, reproducible, and binary. The server is up or it is down. The API returns a 200 or a 500. The database query either executes, or it does not.

The entire operating model of enterprise technology, the roles, the governance, the budgets, the reporting structures, was built around this characteristic. And it worked. Project managers tracked milestones against plans that could be predicted because the system's behaviour was predictable. Testers wrote test cases with expected results because results were expected. Governance boards signed off at defined checkpoints because the checkpoints measured something stable.

This is the water the fish does not see. The assumption is so embedded in how enterprises manage technology that nobody names it. Nobody questions it. It simply is how you deliver technology.

Until the technology changes.

The thirty-year satisfying assumption: *the belief that a system tested is a system finished. It held for every technology that came before AI. It does not hold now.*

WHAT CHANGED

The shift did not arrive with a single product launch or a single year. But it has a shape. For decades, enterprise AI meant rules-based systems and task-specific machine learning models: fraud detection, demand forecasting, recommendation engines. These systems were probabilistic in theory but narrow enough in practice to be governed as if they were deterministic. The inputs were constrained. The outputs were bounded. The variance was manageable within existing frameworks. When large language models moved from research to production, and when agents built on those models began making decisions, planning multi-step actions, and operating with genuine autonomy, the variance stopped being manageable. The delivery model did not notice, because the earlier, narrower version of AI had been manageable within it. The new version is not.

AI systems, and agentic AI systems in particular, do not behave deterministically. They reason. They plan. They act across multiple steps with varying degrees of autonomy. And critically, they produce different outputs from the same inputs depending on context, data state, model updates, and interaction patterns that nobody fully controls.

Consider what this means in practice. A traditional credit decisioning system applies coded rules to an application and produces the same outcome every time: approved, declined, referred. The rules are deterministic. The outcome is auditable. An AI agent evaluating the same application weighs contextual signals, customer history, risk patterns, and policy constraints through probabilistic reasoning. Run it again with the same application, and the recommendation may differ. Not because the system malfunctioned, but because probabilistic reasoning is stochastic by design. The variance is a feature of the architecture, not a bug in the implementation. And when that variance produces a decision a regulator questions, the audit trail looks nothing like the one the compliance team was trained to review.

Jai Ganesh, Chief Product Officer at Harman International and an MIT Sloan Management Review panellist, stated the problem precisely: "Traditional management systems are designed for deterministic systems," whereas agentic AI systems "operate independently, are goal-oriented, and have memory and reasoning capabilities, which make their decisions complex, autonomous, and opaque."

This is not an edge case affecting a small subset of AI deployments. It describes the fundamental operating characteristic of every system that uses a large language model, every agent that makes decisions, and every workflow that involves probabilistic reasoning. The technology that enterprises are deploying at record speed belongs to a different category from the technology their delivery methods were designed for.

Tshilidzi Marwala of the United Nations University reinforced the structural nature of this challenge: "Because of its autonomous decision-making, adaptive learning, and high-speed operations, agentic AI is difficult for traditional management models, which were created for human agency, to handle." David Hardoon of Standard Chartered Bank was blunter: "Old management models, built for human-paced systems, fall short in tracking AI's dynamic behaviour, risking unaddressed errors or harms."

Ganesh, Marwala, and Hardoon arrived at the same conclusion independently. The management models enterprises rely on were not designed for what they are now being asked to manage.

The executives deploying these systems already sense this. An MIT and BCG study of 2,102 executives found that 76% now view agentic AI as "more like a coworker than a tool." That instinct is correct, and it contains the diagnosis. You do not manage a coworker with a Gantt chart. You do not govern a colleague's judgement with a milestone-based review. If three quarters of enterprise leaders already see agents as coworkers, they are acknowledging that the systems they have deployed belong to a different management category from the ones their delivery methods were built for.

MIT SLOAN MANAGEMENT REVIEW / BCG,
The Emerging Agentic Enterprise, November 2025 (2,102 respondents).

WHY NOBODY SAW IT

There is a reason this error is so widespread and so resistant to correction. The deterministic delivery model was not imposed by incompetent leaders. It was built by highly competent ones, over decades, for systems that justified every design choice. The methodology was correct for the systems it was designed for. The systems changed. The methodology did not.

This is a category error, not a competence failure.

The distinction matters because it changes the response. If this were a competence problem, the answer would be training: teach your existing teams to manage AI better. If it is a category error, training within the existing framework makes the problem worse, not better. You cannot train a project manager to manage a probabilistic system using milestones designed for deterministic outcomes. The tool is not broken. It was built for a different job.

McKinsey found that fewer than forty percent of organisations report any enterprise-wide EBIT impact from AI, and most of those attribute less than five percent of EBIT to AI use, despite active adoption across eighty-eight percent of enterprises surveyed. The technology is being deployed. The financial outcomes are not following. Camunda research found that 73% say there is a significant gap between their agentic AI vision and their reality today. These are not organisations that lack AI capability. They are organisations whose management model cannot convert that capability into outcomes. The gap sits precisely where the category error does the most damage: in how the organisation manages, governs, and sustains the system after the technology works.

MCKINSEY,
The State of AI 2025 (1,993 participants, 105 nations), November 2025;
Camunda, 2026 State of Agentic Orchestration & Automation, January 2026 (1,150 leaders).

THE 80/20 SPLIT

Perhaps the clearest evidence of the category error in action comes from MIT. Researchers at ten institutions, deploying an agentic AI system for cancer surveillance in a clinical setting, tracked where their effort actually went. The result inverted every assumption a traditional delivery model would make.

Eighty percent of the effort was not on the AI. It was on data engineering, governance, integration, monitoring, and organisational change. The model itself, the thing most enterprises spend their attention on, consumed roughly twenty percent of the work. The remaining eighty percent fell into categories that no traditional project management framework accounts for: continuous evaluation of probabilistic outputs, governance of autonomous decisions, integration with systems that change independently, and the sociotechnical challenge of embedding an adaptive system into a human organisation.

MIT Sloan's Kate Kellogg, who led the research, described the operational implication: "Organisations need to make monitoring a permanent operational expense, not a one-time project cost." Elsewhere in the same research, she identified the specific challenge: "With agentic AI, these systems are reasoning, planning, and acting independently across multiple steps. So, we need adaptive monitoring, continuously tracking multiple dynamic metrics."

Two phrases in those statements deserve attention. Permanent and adaptive. Traditional delivery assumes that monitoring is a phase: you test, you deploy, you verify, you hand over to operations. Kellogg is describing a system where the monitoring never stops, where the evaluation is continuous, and where static dashboards designed for deterministic systems measure the wrong things entirely. They track uptime when they should track output quality. They measure latency when they should measure drift.

KATE KELLOGG,
MIT Sloan, "5 Heavy Lifts for Agentic AI," February 2026.

A delivery model designed for deterministic systems has no structure for this. It has no role accountable for it. It has no budget category to fund it. And when leaders ask their PMOs why AI systems are failing in production, the PMO can honestly report that the project was delivered on time, on budget, and to specification. The gap between those two statements is the category error.

> *The project succeeded. The system failed. The gap between those two statements is the category error.*

DIMENSION	DETERMINISTIC SYSTEMS	PROBABILISTIC SYSTEMS
Output behaviour	Same input produces same output, every time	Same input produces different outputs depending on context, data state, and upstream conditions
Failure mode	Loud, visible, reproducible. The system is working or it is broken	Silent, cumulative, context dependent. The system degrades before anyone notices
Testing	Test at milestones. If it passes, ship it. Behaviour is stable post-release	Evaluate continuously. Behaviour changes between milestones without code changes
Success metric	On time, on budget, to specification	Is the system healthy, safe, economically viable, and performing as expected right now?
Economic model	Project budget with a defined return period	Operating expenditure that must be tracked at the level of individual tasks
Completion	The project closes. The team moves on	The system is never finished. Deployment is the first day of operations, not the last
Management approach	Project management: milestone-based governance with a defined end state	System stewardship: continuous evaluation, governance, and adaptation

Every row in this table represents a management assumption that must change. Most enterprises have changed none of them.

FIGURE 2.1
Deterministic vs Probabilistic Systems

THE PMO REFLEX

The natural response to this diagnosis is that existing teams can absorb the difference. The PMO has managed complexity before. DevOps already handles production operations. SRE already monitors system health. The instinct is to say: we do not need a new discipline, we need our existing disciplines to try harder.

This instinct is understandable. It is also the category error restating itself.

DevOps manages infrastructure reliability: servers, containers, deployment pipelines. It does not manage whether the output of a customer-facing agent is accurate, appropriate, or economically viable. SRE manages system uptime and latency. It does not manage whether a system that is fully operational is producing outputs that are slowly drifting away from their intended quality. Project management tracks delivery against a plan. It has no mechanism for tracking a system that changes its own behaviour without code changes, budget changes, or plan changes.

The adaptive monitoring that Kellogg described requires something none of these functions were built to provide: continuous evaluation of probabilistic outputs against shifting baselines. Static monitoring dashboards designed for deterministic systems track uptime when they should track output quality. They measure latency when they should measure drift. They report system health when the system is healthy by every infrastructure metric but producing outputs that are silently degrading.

Asking your PMO, your DevOps team, or your SRE function to manage AI systems is not wrong because these teams are incompetent. It is wrong because their tools, processes, and mental models were designed for a category of system that behaves fundamentally differently. Giving them more resources to do the same job better will produce more precisely tracked projects that still fail in production.

THE FALSE CONFIDENCE PROBLEM

There is a consequence of the category error that is worse than failure. It is false confidence.

When an enterprise applies deterministic delivery methods to a probabilistic system, the delivery process produces results that look correct by every established measure. The project passes its governance gates. The testing phase reports acceptable results because the tests were designed for deterministic outcomes. The budget tracking shows the project is within tolerance. The milestone reviews confirm progress. Everything that the organisation measures tell leadership that the system is ready.

It is not. The governance gates did not test for output variability under production conditions. The tests measured accuracy against a static dataset, not performance against real-world input that shifts daily. The budget did not account for per-task operating costs that compound unpredictably. The milestones measured delivery progress, not production readiness.

The pattern is recognisable. A customer-facing agent is deployed after a successful pilot. The steering committee sees the pilot metrics in a board presentation. The numbers look strong: high accuracy, fast response times, positive user feedback. The governance review signs off. Three weeks into production, a customer receives a response that is confidently wrong. Not a system crash, not an outage, but a fluent, authoritative answer that happens to be incorrect. The incident triggers an investigation. The investigation reveals that the agent's output quality had been drifting since week one, producing progressively less reliable responses as real-world input diverged from the controlled test data. Nothing in the monitoring infrastructure was designed to detect this. The dashboards tracked uptime, latency, and throughput. The agent scored perfectly on all three. It was also giving customers wrong answers.

When the CIO asks how the governance review missed it, the answer is uncomfortable: it did not miss anything. It measured everything it was designed to measure. The governance framework was designed for a system whose outputs do not change after deployment. Nobody asked whether the outputs were still accurate, because in the deterministic model, that question does not need to be asked.

The system enters production. And then it begins to change, in ways nobody is watching, using metrics nobody defined, with consequences nobody owns. The project manager has moved to the next project. The test team has been redeployed. The governance board signed off six weeks ago. Nobody is accountable for what the system does after deployment, because in the deterministic model, what a system does after deployment is what it did before deployment.

Applying the old model harder does not close this gap. It widens it. More rigorous project management produces more precisely documented projects that still fail in production. More thorough testing against deterministic criteria produces higher confidence in results that do not predict production behaviour. More detailed governance signoffs create a more complete paper trail documenting the moment the organisation formally approved a system it did not understand.

WHERE IT BREAKS

The category error is not an abstract diagnostic. It has concrete, measurable consequences that propagate through every management structure the enterprise relies on.

Start with staffing. Enterprises assign project managers to AI initiatives and expect them to manage systems that behave nothing like projects. No role exists to own system health in production, because the delivery model assumes health is stable after deployment. The role gap is not an oversight. It is a design assumption inherited from thirty years of deterministic systems where health after deployment was, in fact, stable.

The budget architecture carries the same assumption. AI gets funded as a capital project with a defined return period. Then the operating costs arrive: ongoing, variable, tied to per-task economics that no project budget can predict or govern. The CFO sees a cost category that does not fit any existing line item. It is not infrastructure. It is not headcount. It is the cost of running a probabilistic system, and no template in the finance function was designed to capture it.

Governance suffers a different version of the same problem. Milestone-based review assumes that what passes the gate stays passed. A governance board approves the system on Wednesday. The system drifts on Thursday. Nobody reviews again until the next scheduled gate, three months away. The governance framework functioned exactly as designed. It was designed for a system that does not change between gates.

Then there is accountability. The project team built the system. The project closed. Operations inherited something they do not have the AI-specific capability to evaluate. The gap between the team that understands the system and the team that runs it is a direct consequence of the project-based model, which assumes a clean handover is possible because the system is finished. AI systems are never finished.

The cumulative result is visible in every data set that measures enterprise AI outcomes. These are not technology failure rates. They are delivery model failure rates. The technology works. The method of managing it does not.

THE EXPLANATIONS THAT DO NOT COMPETE

Enterprise leaders who recognise the pattern described above will often point to a different explanation for why their AI programme underperformed. The data was fragmented. The talent was not available. The legacy systems would not integrate. The executive sponsor moved on. These are not wrong observations. They are genuine enterprise pain points and dismissing them would be dishonest.

But trace each one to its structural root, and it leads to the same place.

Fragmented data is not a data problem. It is a delivery model problem. Deterministic delivery assumes data is cleaned once during the build phase and remains stable after deployment. Probabilistic systems require continuous data quality because the system's behaviour changes with its inputs. The enterprise has no operational practice for ongoing data health because the delivery model never required one. The data is fragmented because nobody was funded, staffed, or accountable for maintaining it after the project closed.

Talent gaps are not a hiring problem. They are a role architecture problem. The roles needed to steward probabilistic systems do not exist in the deterministic organisational chart. Enterprises are not failing to fill positions. They are trying to fill positions that were designed for a different type of system. The talent gap is a design consequence, not a recruitment failure.

Legacy integration is not a technology problem. It is a governance model problem. Deterministic integration is a point-in-time event: connect the systems, test the connection, move on. Probabilistic integration requires continuous monitoring because the AI system's behaviour shifts while the legacy system stays fixed. The integration breaks not because it was built badly but because nobody was watching it after the project team moved on.

Executive sponsorship gaps are not a leadership problem. They are a metrics problem. When the delivery model reports project completion as success, the executive moves on to the next initiative. Probabilistic systems need ongoing executive attention because the system has not finished performing when the project finishes building. The sponsor's attention followed the metrics. The metrics were designed for a system that ends.

The pattern is the same every time. The enterprise names a specific challenge. The challenge is real. But when you trace it back, it leads to a delivery model that was designed for systems that stay fixed after deployment being applied to systems that do not. These explanations do not compete with the category error. They are consequences of it. They are what the category error looks like when it shows up in the data team, the HR function, the integration architecture, and the executive calendar.

This is what makes the structural diagnosis different from a list of problems to solve. Fixing the data without changing the delivery model produces cleaner data that nobody maintains after the project closes. Hiring AI talent without changing the role architecture places capable people in roles that measure the wrong things. Upgrading legacy integration without changing the governance model produces better connections that nobody monitors after deployment. Each fix addresses a symptom and leaves the structural cause intact.

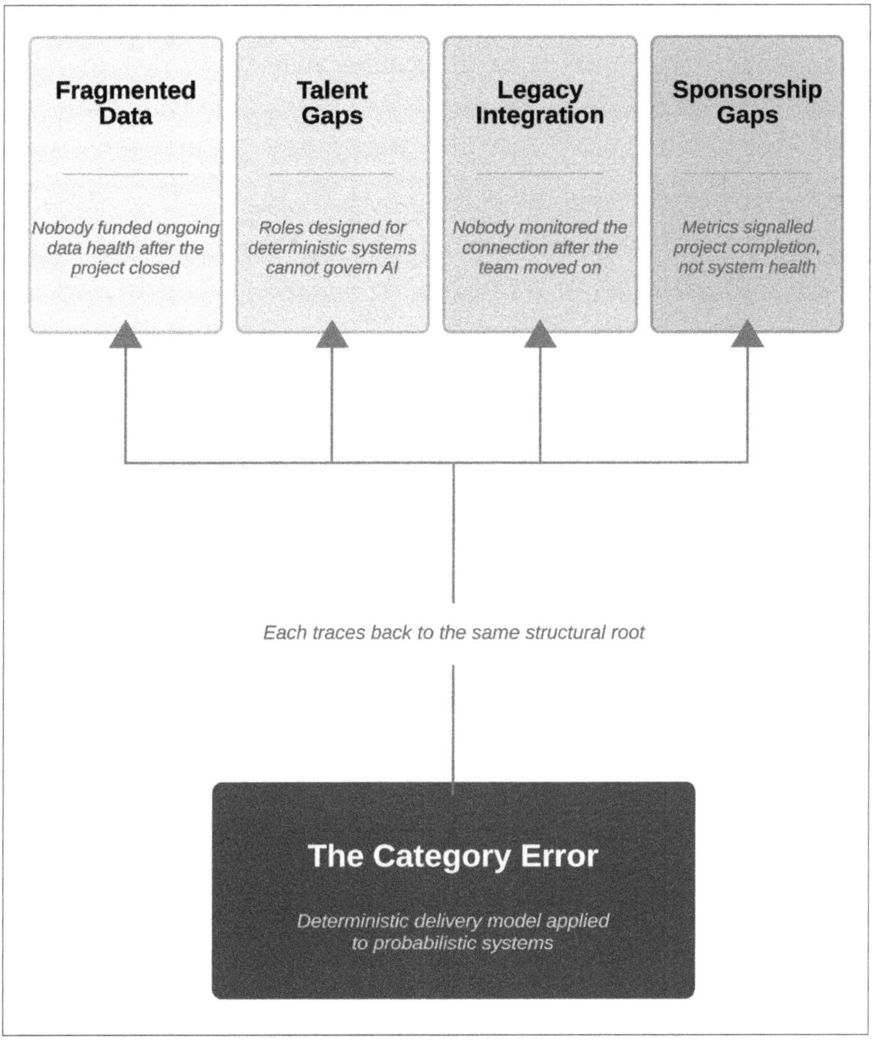

The category error does not sit alongside the usual explanations for AI failure. It sits underneath all of them.

Four common explanations for enterprise AI failure. Each is real. Each traces to the same structural root: a delivery model designed for deterministic systems applied without modification to probabilistic ones.

FIGURE 2.2
The Explanations That Do Not Compete

The category error is not the only factor in enterprise AI failure. Technology limitations are real. Use case selection matters. Organisational readiness varies. But none of these factors explain why the failure rate is structural and worsening. Bad use cases can be selected away. Technology limitations improve with each model generation. Organisational readiness can be built. The category error persists because it is invisible. It is embedded in every methodology, every governance framework, and every budget template the enterprise relies on. The other factors are problems to solve. The category error is the lens that must be replaced before solving them produces lasting results.

WHAT THIS MEANS

If the diagnosis is correct, the response is clear. The answer is not to apply deterministic delivery methods more rigorously to probabilistic systems. The answer is to replace the management model with one that was designed for how these systems actually behave.

That replacement is system stewardship: the ongoing practice of monitoring, evaluating, governing, and adapting AI systems in production. Not as an add-on to existing project management, but as a different discipline designed for a fundamentally different kind of system.

The category error is sharpest where autonomy is highest. A constrained retrieval system with deterministic guardrails faces a milder version of the mismatch. A multi-step autonomous agent making decisions across workflows faces the full force of it. The discipline described in this book scales to both, but the urgency scales with autonomy.

Every enterprise leader who has felt the frustration of watching well-funded AI initiatives fail despite competent teams and proven technology now has a structural explanation for what happened. It was not bad execution. It was the wrong category.

The question that follows is practical: if the current model is wrong, what replaces it? What does a delivery discipline designed for probabilistic systems actually look like? Who is accountable for system health after deployment? How do you govern something that changes without permission? These are not theoretical questions. They are the questions that determine whether the next AI investment produces outcomes or produces another well-documented failure.

AI systems do not fail loudly.
They degrade silently,
behind dashboards
that say everything is fine.

VIJAYAN SEENISAMY

CHAPTER 3

Five Ways Enterprise AI Fails

The diagnosis is structural. A delivery model designed for deterministic systems, applied without modification to technology that behaves probabilistically. But a diagnosis is not a map.

The executive who presents this to their board will hear the same question: where exactly is it breaking? The answer is five specific places, each predictable, each preventable, and each currently invisible to the management structures most enterprises rely on.

THE DEMO GOD CURSE

Every enterprise that has deployed AI has a version of this story. The pilot was a success. The numbers were strong. Leadership approved the move to production. Within weeks, the system that had performed flawlessly began producing outputs that ranged from subtly wrong to visibly embarrassing. The team scrambles. The investigation reveals nothing broken in the technical sense. The system is operating exactly as designed. It is simply operating in an environment that the pilot never tested.

The Demo God Curse is the most visceral of the five failure modes because it is the one that reaches the board. Air Canada was held legally responsible for misinformation generated by its customer chatbot, a system that had been tested, approved, and deployed through the organisation's standard governance process. Commonwealth Bank reversed its AI voice system after a public failure that demonstrated how quickly cost savings evaporate when the deployment decision outpaces operational reality. Klarna replaced 700 customer service roles with AI over two years, then began rehiring after customer satisfaction declined. McDonald's AI hiring chatbot left 64 million job applications vulnerable to exposure because the governance model delegated accountability to a vendor without verifying the vendor's security practices.

Air Canada, Commonwealth Bank, Klarna, and McDonald's. Different industries. The same structural failure.

The curse operates through a specific mechanism. Pilot conditions are artificially optimised in ways that production cannot replicate. The data is curated. The volume is low. The edge cases are few. The team that built the system is in the room, monitoring every interaction and correcting problems in real time. When the system moves to production, every one of those conditions inverts. The data arrives from systems the pilot never tested against. Volume scales by orders of magnitude and exposes failure modes that low-volume testing never surfaced. The builder moves to the next project. Nobody replaces them.

DIMENSION	PILOT CONDITIONS	PRODUCTION REALITY
Data	Curated, clean, representative samples selected by the build team	Unfiltered, messy, edge cases from systems never tested against
Volume	Tens to hundreds of interactions, manageable review by humans	Thousands to millions, impossible to review individually
Oversight	Build team in the room, monitoring every interaction, correcting in real time	Build team moved to next project. No dedicated oversight role assigned
Edge cases	Few and manageable. Testing covers the expected range of inputs	Exponentially more. Users find inputs the test suite never imagined
Environment	Controlled, isolated, stable infrastructure with known dependencies	Connected to live systems, upstream changes arrive without warning
Governance	Informal, embedded in the team. Problems fixed before anyone notices	Formal processes required. Nobody designed them for this system

FIGURE 3.1
The Demo God Curse: Pilot vs Production Conditions

The curse is not that the demo was dishonest. It is that the demo was accurate, under conditions that production will never replicate. And because the demo was accurate, it became the evidence on which the organisation made its investment decision, staffed its support model, and designed its governance. The stronger the demo, the less prepared the organisation is for what follows.

> ***The Demo God Curse:*** *the better the pilot performs, the less prepared the organisation is for production. The demo creates the confidence. Production reveals the cost.*

DRIFT WITHOUT DETECTION

The Demo God Curse is loud. It produces an incident that forces a response. Drift is silent. It is the failure mode that accumulates for weeks or months before anyone notices, and by the time it becomes visible, the damage has compounded to the point where recovery is expensive and trust has eroded.

Drift in a probabilistic system is not a malfunction. It is a characteristic. The model's behaviour shifts as the data environment changes, as upstream systems update, as user interaction patterns evolve. In a deterministic system, this would trigger an alert because the output would deviate from the coded specification. In a probabilistic system, the output quality shifts gradually, and the monitoring infrastructure, if it was designed for deterministic systems, does not measure output quality at all. It sees uptime, latency, and error codes. It does not see accuracy declining. The dashboards show green. The latency is within tolerance. The system is fully operational. The outputs are getting progressively worse.

Consider what drift looks like from the inside. A customer support agent is deployed with a 94% accuracy rate established during the pilot. The team celebrates. The project closes. Over the next six weeks, the accuracy slides to 88%, then 82%. No code changed. No configuration was altered. The data flowing into the system shifted because a product update changed the kinds of questions customers were asking, and the agent's responses drifted outside the calibration it was built on. The engineering dashboards show the system is fully operational. Response times are within tolerance. The infrastructure is healthy. Nobody knows the outputs are degrading because the monitoring was designed to detect system failure, not output quality decline.

MIT researchers deploying agentic AI in clinical settings confirmed that continuous adaptive monitoring was essential precisely because static monitoring designed for deterministic systems could not detect this kind of drift. The monitoring had to track multiple dynamic metrics simultaneously, not just infrastructure health. Kate Kellogg of MIT Sloan described the implication: monitoring for AI systems must be a permanent operational expense, not a one-time project cost.

LangChain surveyed over 1,300 AI practitioners and found that 89% of organisations had implemented some form of observability for their agents. That number sounds reassuring until the next finding: only 52% run formal evaluations. The tooling exists. The discipline to use it systematically does not.

> *Observability without evaluation is an instrument panel that nobody reads.*
>
> **LANGCHAIN,**
> State of Agent Engineering, December 2025 (1,300+ professionals).

The financial consequence of undetected drift is not the cost of fixing the system. It is the cost of the decisions that were made using degraded outputs during the weeks or months before anyone noticed. A customer-facing agent whose accuracy drifts from 94% to 82% over six weeks has produced thousands of interactions at declining quality. A lead-scoring agent whose calibration shifts has mispriced hundreds of opportunities. A regulatory filing assistant whose outputs drift has submitted documents that may not withstand scrutiny. None of these triggered an alert because the monitoring was watching uptime, not output quality.

The CFO experiences drift as a business case that stops delivering. The business case assumed a sustained level of performance. When drift degrades that performance without detection, the returns the business case predicted do not materialise, and the finance team cannot explain why because the system was never reported as failing.

GOVERNANCE THEATRE

IBM's 2025 data breach research produced a finding that should alarm every CIO in the room: among organisations that experienced an AI-related security incident, 97% lacked proper AI access controls. Sixty-three percent of all breached organisations lacked AI governance policies entirely. The systems were in production. The governance was not.

IBM,
2025 Data Breach Report.

This is governance theatre: the appearance of governance without the operational substance to detect, prevent, or respond to the failure modes that probabilistic systems produce. The governance framework exists. The documentation is complete. The review boards meet on schedule. And the governance measures nothing that actually matters for an AI system in production.

Governance theatre has a specific anatomy. The review board evaluates the system at deployment against criteria designed for deterministic software: does it meet the specification, has it passed testing, is the documentation complete. The system passes because these questions have verifiable answers. But nobody asks whether the system's outputs will remain accurate after deployment, whether the governance framework includes continuous evaluation, or whether anyone is accountable for the system's behaviour between review cycles. The governance signed off on a snapshot. The system moved.

The gap between what governance measures and what production produces is where governance theatre lives. Governance asks: does the system conform to specification? Production needs to know: is the system still performing within acceptable parameters right now? Governance asks: has the system been tested? Production needs: is the testing regime continuous, or did it end at deployment? Governance asks: who signed off? Production needs: who is accountable for what the system does next Tuesday?

Deloitte surveyed 3,235 leaders across 24 countries and found that only one in five had a mature model for governance of autonomous AI agents. The correlation between governance maturity and business value was clear: enterprises where senior leadership actively shapes AI governance achieve significantly greater results. But four out of five enterprises have not built that governance model. They have built a version of it designed for a different kind of system and applied it to AI without changing the questions it asks.

DELOITTE,
State of AI in the Enterprise 2026 (3,235 leaders, 24 countries).

The regulatory dimension makes governance theatre more dangerous than the leadership teams running it may realise. The EU AI Act is now in force with enforcement mechanisms that include fines of up to 3% of global turnover for non-compliance in high-risk AI systems, and up to 7% for prohibited practices. The Colorado AI Act created the first comprehensive US state-level compliance framework with specific requirements for preventing algorithmic discrimination, including mandatory impact assessments. These regulations do not ask whether an enterprise has a governance framework. They ask whether the framework produces auditable evidence of continuous compliance. Governance theatre cannot survive a regulatory inquiry because it measures the wrong things. The documentation is complete. The evidence of ongoing monitoring, continuous evaluation, and production-level accountability is not, because the governance model was never designed to produce it.

The danger of governance theatre is that it is worse than no governance at all. No governance produces visible chaos. The CIO knows there is a problem because the incidents are unmanaged. Governance theatre produces invisible degradation behind a wall of documentation that tells leadership everything is under control. When the failure eventually surfaces, it is larger than it needed to be, it has been accumulating longer than anyone knew, and the governance framework that was supposed to prevent it has a complete paper trail showing it was functioning correctly throughout.

> *Governance theatre is worse than no governance at all. No governance produces visible chaos that demands a response. Governance theatre produces invisible degradation behind a wall of documentation that says everything is under control.*

FRAGMENTED ACCOUNTABILITY

Ask a simple question about any AI agent in production at a large enterprise: who is accountable for this system's health right now?

In a typical enterprise, the answer requires a conversation. The project manager built it. The project closed. The engineering team maintains the infrastructure. Operations handle incidents, if the incident is the kind of thing they know how to handle. The business owner who requested the system has moved on to the next initiative. The CAIO may or may not know the system exists. Nobody is wrong. Nobody is failing at their job. The accountability structure was designed for a project that ends, and the system is something that does not.

This is not an oversight. It is a design feature of the project-based delivery model. When a project closes, accountability transfers to operations. For deterministic software, this transfer works because the thing being transferred is stable. The operations team can manage it with standard procedures. For AI systems, the transfer creates an accountability vacuum. The team that understands how the system was designed, what trade-offs were made, what calibration decisions shaped its behaviour, has moved on. The team that inherits it does not have the AI-specific capability to evaluate whether the system is still performing as intended.

The result is predictable. When something goes wrong, the response is reactive and ad hoc. Whoever notices the problem first becomes the owner by default, regardless of whether they have the authority or capability to resolve it. Prompt updates are made without governance review. Configuration changes happen without communication to downstream teams. In one enterprise assessment, fourteen prompt updates to a single production agent in a single quarter, none governed, directly caused a twelve percent accuracy decline. The decline was detected by users, not by the team.

Fragmented accountability compounds across a portfolio. Managing one AI agent with ad hoc accountability is uncomfortable but survivable. Managing ten agents this way produces conflicting priorities, duplicated effort, and an inability to make portfolio-level decisions about where to invest and what to deprecate. Managing fifty creates a governance crisis that no amount of individual heroism can resolve. The CAIO becomes the single point of failure for the entire portfolio because nobody else has the authority or the context to make decisions, and the CAIO does not have the operational infrastructure to make those decisions at scale.

NEGATIVE UNIT ECONOMICS

The four failure modes above destroy trust, create risk, and erode performance. This one destroys the business case.

Negative unit economics is the condition where an AI agent costs more per task than the human process it was deployed to replace. It sounds like a simple measurement problem. It is not. It is a structural consequence of the project-based funding model, which budgets AI as a capital investment with a projected return and then has no mechanism to track operating costs at the level where they actually compound.

Enterprise AI agents cost between $3,200 and $13,000 per month to operate in production. That range includes compute, API and inference costs, human oversight, and allocated infrastructure. The variance is enormous because token-based pricing fluctuates with context length, retry behaviour, and interaction patterns that no project budget can predict. A minor change in how users interact with the system, a slightly longer average query, a higher retry rate when the system is uncertain, can double inference costs without any change to the system itself.

CB Insights surveyed 59 executives and found that 40% admitted they could not track, or were unaware of, the actual return on investment for their AI agents. Forty percent. These are enterprises that approved business cases with projected returns, deployed systems with approved budgets, and then lost visibility into whether the economics still hold. The project budget was spent. The operating costs arrived. The finance function had no template to capture them because AI operating costs do not fit any existing budget category. They are not infrastructure. They are not headcount. They are the cost of running a probabilistic system, and the financial governance model was not designed for them.

The total cost of ownership for AI systems is underestimated by 40 to 60 percent in most enterprise deployments. The visible costs, the ones that appeared in the business case, are the model, the compute, and the integration. The invisible costs are ongoing: monitoring, evaluation, human oversight, governance, and the compound operating expense of per-task token consumption at production scale. The business case modelled the visible half. The invisible half showed up as a budget surprise that the CFO's team had no framework to anticipate, because no previous technology category had this cost structure.

Australian data makes the scale of the problem concrete. ADAPT's research across Australian CFOs found that finance leaders estimate 40% of deployed technology in organisations goes unused. That figure covers all enterprise technology, not just AI. For AI programmes where nobody can track cost per task, where the operating expense has no line item, and where the finance function has no mechanism to distinguish a productive inference call from a wasted retry, the waste rate is almost certainly higher. The 40% is the baseline. AI without economic governance sits above it.

ADAPT,
CFO Edge Research, November 2025.

THE COMPOUND PROBLEM

These five failure modes do not operate independently. They reinforce each other in ways that accelerate the damage and make it harder to diagnose.

An agent that drifts without detection (failure mode two) will eventually trigger the Demo God Curse (failure mode one) when the degradation becomes visible to customers or regulators. The investigation will reveal that the governance framework did not detect the drift (failure mode three) because nobody was accountable for monitoring it (failure mode four). The cost analysis will show that the agent had been operating at negative unit economics for months (failure mode five), but nobody had visibility into the per-task costs because the financial governance model was designed for project budgets, not operating expenditure.

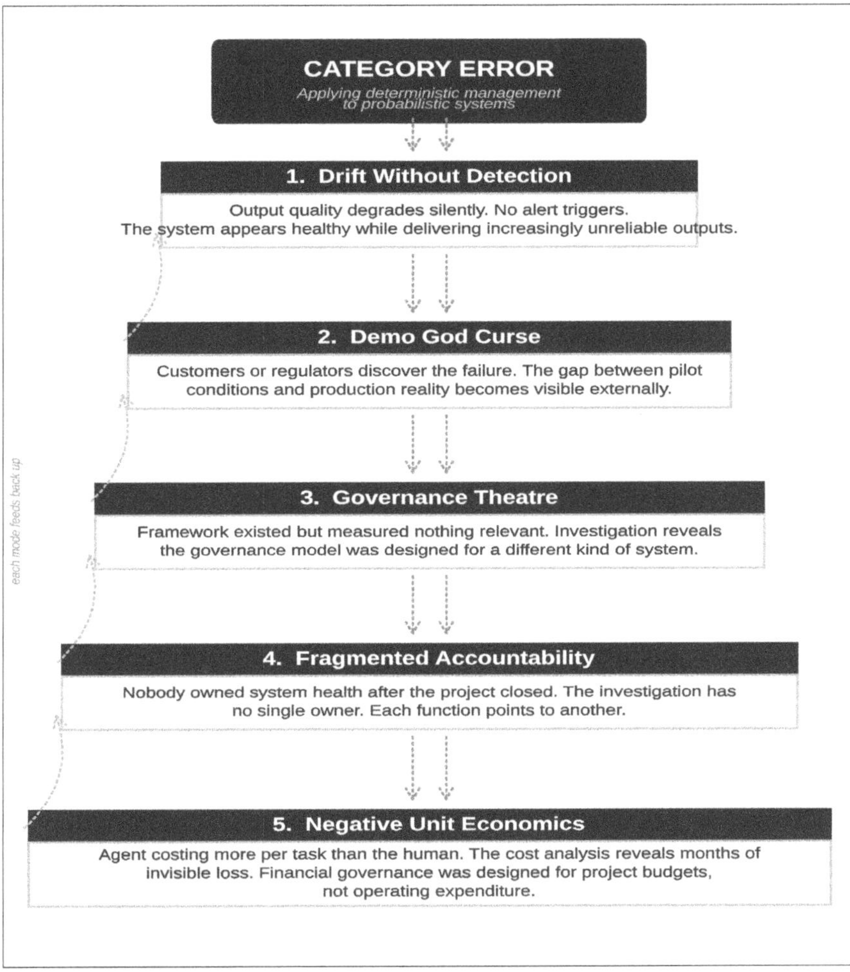

Each layer widens because each failure mode amplifies the damage surface of the next. Any failure mode can be the entry point. The cascade flows from whichever fracture appears first

FIGURE 3.2
How the Five Failure Modes Compound

This is not a hypothetical sequence. It is the pattern that the Air Canada, Commonwealth Bank, Klarna, and McDonald's incidents each followed, in different orders and with different failure modes as the entry point. The compounding happens because the failures are connected through the same root cause: a delivery model that does not measure, govern, or manage the dimensions that probabilistic systems require.

The compounding effect matters for two reasons. First, it means that addressing any single failure mode in isolation provides limited protection. An enterprise that invests in observability (to catch drift) but does not invest in accountability (to act on what the observability detects) has bought instruments that nobody reads. An enterprise that fixes accountability but ignores economic governance has a team watching a system bleed money without the tools to quantify the damage. Second, it means that the total risk exposure of an unmanaged AI portfolio is not the sum of the individual agent risks. It is the product of their interactions. A portfolio of ten agents, each with undetected drift, each with fragmented accountability, each without continuous governance, creates a risk surface that is qualitatively different from the risk of any single agent.

McKinsey's research across nearly two thousand participants in 105 nations found that the majority of organisations deploying AI agents were doing so with no formal governance oversight. That finding is worth sitting with. Not small enterprises experimenting at the margins. Sophisticated, well-funded organisations staffed with capable people, operating AI agents in production without the governance structures to detect when those agents fail. The five failure modes described in this chapter are not theoretical risks. They are currently operating, right now, at scale, across industries, in organisations that do not yet have the language to describe what is happening or the framework to prevent it.

MCKINSEY,
The State of AI 2025 (1,993 participants, 105 nations), November 2025.

THE BETTER MODELS OBJECTION

The natural response from technology-focused leadership is that better models will solve these problems. Model accuracy is improving. Context windows are expanding. Hallucination rates are declining. The technology is getting better every quarter. This is true. It is also irrelevant to the diagnosis.

Starbucks has operated AI in production for seven years across personalisation, inventory, staffing, and store operations. As their AI capabilities expanded, they needed more operational discipline, not less. Better models did not reduce their need for MLOps, monitoring, and cross-functional governance. Better models increased it, because more capable systems operating across more business functions created more complexity that required more sophisticated operational management.

BCG's research confirmed the structural point: ten percent of the challenge in enterprise AI is the technology itself, twenty percent is the data, and seventy percent is people and processes. Better models address the ten percent. The five failure modes in this chapter live in the seventy percent. Model improvement is real and welcome. It does not address drift detection, governance design, accountability structures, economic governance, or the operational discipline that determines whether a working system produces enterprise outcomes.

The enterprises that are getting results are not the ones with the best models. They are the ones that have built the operational infrastructure to sustain whatever models they have. The discipline came before the results, not after.

WHAT THESE FAILURES TELL YOU

Every one of these failure modes is preventable. Not with better technology. With better delivery discipline.

The Demo God Curse is prevented by evaluating AI systems under production conditions before deployment decisions are made, not under the curated conditions that made the pilot look flawless. Drift is prevented by continuous evaluation that measures output quality, not just infrastructure health. Governance theatre is prevented by building governance for probabilistic systems that asks different questions than governance for deterministic software. Fragmented accountability is prevented by designing roles and structures where someone owns system health after the project closes. Negative unit economics is prevented by tracking cost per task from the first day of production, not discovering it when the CFO asks why the AI budget has tripled.

Each prevention mechanism maps to one of the five control surfaces described later in this book. This is not a coincidence. The control surfaces were designed as the structural response to these failure modes. The diagnosis and the solution are two sides of the same architecture.

The pattern was consistent. The business case captured the build cost. The steering committee approved it. What nobody had modelled was the operating cost of a system that consumes resources on every single task, at a rate that fluctuates with variables no project budget template has a field for.

A DIFFERENT KIND OF COST

Traditional enterprise technology follows a predictable financial arc. You invest capital upfront to build or buy the system. You budget a known operating cost to run it. The variance between forecast and actual is small because the cost drivers are stable: licensing fees, infrastructure, headcount, maintenance windows. A financial controller can model a three-year run rate with reasonable confidence because the cost structure is deterministic. The system costs roughly the same to run in month twelve as it does in month one.

AI systems invert this pattern. The build cost is the smaller number. Enterprise AI agents cost between $75,000 and $500,000 to develop, depending on complexity, integration depth, and the regulatory environment they operate in. Integration engineering and safety testing alone consume 40 to 60 percent of that build investment. Those are large numbers, but they are knowable. They appear in the business case. They are approved through normal capital expenditure processes. The finance team understands them because they behave like every other technology investment the organisation has ever made.

The operating cost is where the financial model breaks. The per-agent monthly costs documented in the previous chapter,

$3,200 to $13,000, represent only the visible portion. The range itself is the problem. A CFO can budget for a licensing fee because it arrives as a fixed number on a predictable schedule. A CFO cannot budget for a cost that shifts based on how users interact with the system, how long their queries run, how often the model retries a failed response, and whether upstream data changes trigger reprocessing cycles the original business case never anticipated.

The mechanism is worth understanding because it explains why the cost is ungovernable under current financial models. For enterprises using commercial AI APIs, token-based pricing means the vendor charges per unit of text processed, both inbound and outbound. Enterprises running open-source or self-hosted models avoid vendor token charges but absorb equivalent variability through GPU compute, memory, and inference infrastructure costs that scale with the same unpredictable patterns. Context length determines cost per call: a simple query and a complex query to the same model can differ in cost by an order of magnitude, and the organisation has no control over which type of query users submit. Retry behaviour adds a hidden multiplier. When the model produces a low-confidence response and the system automatically retries, the organisation pays for both the failed attempt and the successful one. Neither appears as a separate line item. A minor change in prompt structure or application usage can double inference costs overnight. No configuration changed. No new feature was deployed. Users simply started asking slightly different questions, and the token consumption pattern shifted in ways that the monitoring infrastructure, designed for deterministic workloads, could not explain.

Traditional monitoring tools track compute consumed. They do not track why. They cannot distinguish between a productive inference call that served a customer and a wasted retry that served nobody. GPUs are scarce, bursty, and expensive. The cost is not just variable. It is variable in ways that have no precedent in enterprise technology budgeting, because no previous technology category coupled per-transaction pricing with unpredictable transaction complexity.

A worked example makes the inversion concrete. Consider a customer service triage agent deployed to classify and route inbound enquiries. During the pilot, the agent handles 200 enquiries per day. Each enquiry averages 800 input tokens and 400 output tokens. At a blended rate of $0.01 per 1,000 tokens, the daily inference cost is approximately $2.40. The pilot business case compares this against a human agent processing the same 200 enquiries at a fully loaded cost of $35 per hour across a four-hour shift: $140 per day. The economics are compelling. The agent costs less than two percent of the human baseline.

In production, the same agent handles 5,000 enquiries per day. The arithmetic should scale linearly: 25 times the volume, 25 times the cost, still dramatically cheaper than 25 times the human baseline. It does not. Complex enquiries that were rare at 200 per day appear hundreds of times at 5,000. Average token consumption per enquiry rises from 1,200 to 2,800 as the agent encounters longer conversations, ambiguous inputs, and multi-step classification chains. Retry rates climb from 3% to 11% as edge cases trigger confidence thresholds. The daily inference cost is no longer $60 (the linear projection) but $172. Add the observability infrastructure ($85/day amortised), the human review queue for low-confidence classifications ($280/day for a part-time senior agent), and the governance overhead for a customer-facing system in a regulated industry ($45/day amortised). The actual daily operating cost is $582.

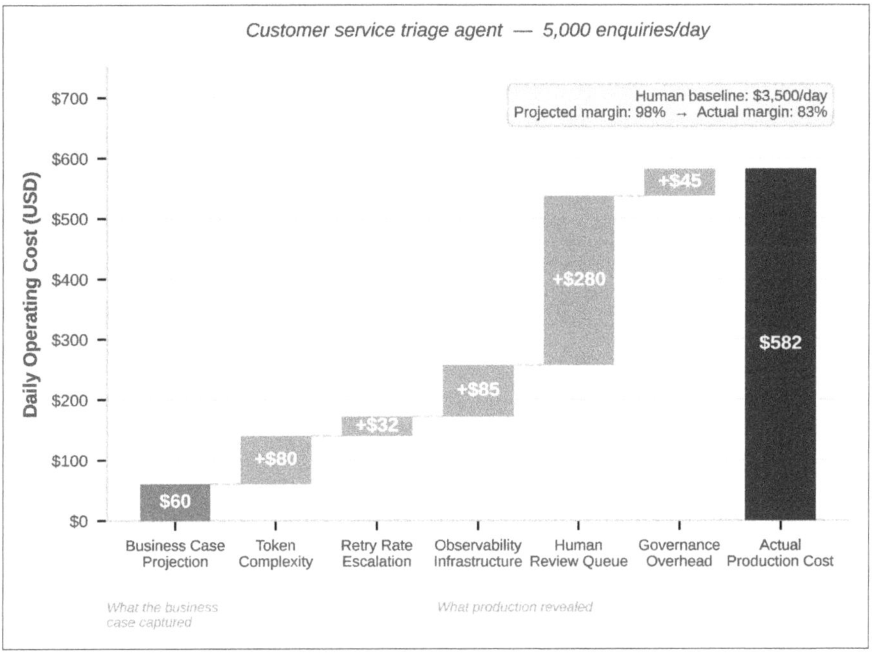

FIGURE 4.1
The Cost the Business Case Missed

The human baseline for 5,000 enquiries is approximately $3,500 per day across a team of six agents. The AI agent is still cheaper. But the margin has collapsed from 98% in the pilot to 83% in production, and nobody in the finance function has visibility into the trajectory. If retry rates continue to climb, if the model provider increases pricing, if regulatory requirements add another review layer, the margin narrows further. The point at which the agent costs more per task than the human process it replaced is not a theoretical risk. It is a mathematical boundary that moves closer every time a variable shifts, and nothing in the enterprise's financial governance is designed to detect when it crosses.

Klarna discovered this boundary publicly. In 2023, the company replaced 700 customer service agents with an AI assistant, claiming it handled two thirds of all customer interactions. The visible cost saving was immediate. By mid-2025, the CEO publicly admitted the company had "focused too much on efficiency and cost." Customer satisfaction had declined, service quality was inconsistent, and the company began rehiring human agents. The economics that justified the deployment did not account for the economics of operating it. The savings were real in the pilot arithmetic. The costs that erased them were invisible in the business case: declining quality, rising escalation rates, brand erosion, and the rehiring expense of reversing a workforce decision made on incomplete cost data.

The governance cost arrives last and surprises the most. When security and compliance requirements surface mid-deployment, and they always do in regulated industries, the budget increase runs between 20 and 30 percent above the original estimate. Observability infrastructure alone adds $500 to $10,000 per month per agent, depending on data volume: logging pipelines, vector database hosting, embedding generation, and the evaluation tooling required to determine whether the agent is still performing within acceptable boundaries.

Add the annual maintenance burden. Industry analyses document ongoing maintenance at 15 to 25 percent of the initial development cost per year. For an agent that cost $300,000 to build, that is $45,000 to $75,000 annually in maintenance alone, before a single inference call is made.

THE ICEBERG

The business case for most enterprise AI deployments captures the visible costs: the model, the compute, the integration. These are the numbers that appear in the investment proposal, the numbers the steering committee reviews, the numbers the finance team tracks.

Below the waterline sits everything the business case missed. Monitoring. Evaluation. Human oversight. Governance and compliance. Drift correction. Retraining. In some deployments, the cost of evaluating an agent's outputs, using a second model to judge the first, exceeds the cost of running the agent itself. This cost category appears in no enterprise business case. The compound operating expense of per-task token consumption at production scale. These costs do not arrive in a single invoice. They accumulate across months, distributed across budget categories that were not designed to capture them, until the total exceeds the original build cost and nobody can explain precisely where the money went.

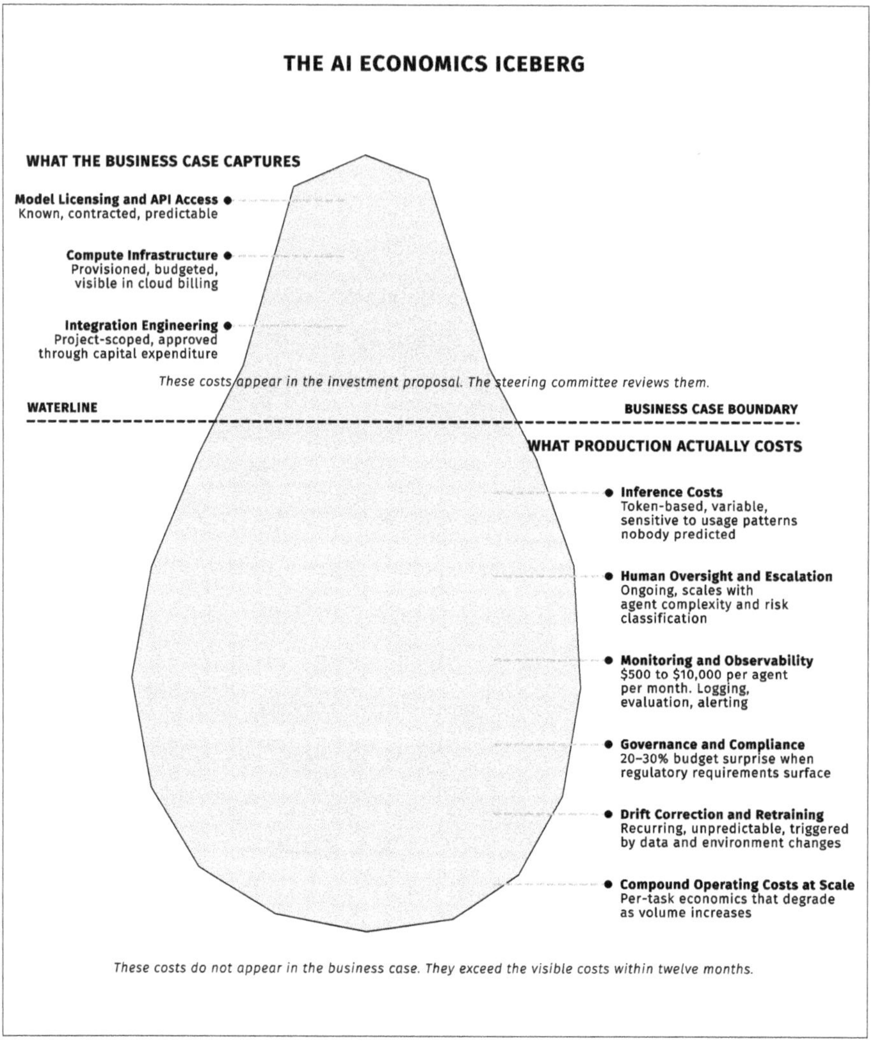

Above the waterline: what the business case captured. Below the waterline: what production actually costs.

FIGURE 4.2
The AI Economics Iceberg

The iceberg is not a metaphor for hidden fees. It is a structural description of a cost model that no previous enterprise technology category has produced. Software licensing is predictable. Cloud infrastructure scales in known increments. Even large-scale data platforms follow cost curves that a finance team can model from historical usage patterns. AI operating costs follow none of these patterns. They are consumption-based, variable, compounding, and sensitive to behavioural changes that occur outside the technology team's control.

A directional planning ratio emerges from the data across this chapter. Build costs for enterprise AI agents run $75,000 to $500,000. Monthly operating costs per agent, documented earlier in this chapter, compound further when governance, observability, and maintenance are included. Annual maintenance adds 15 to 25 percent of the build cost. TCO is underestimated by 40 to 60 percent in most business cases. Taken together, a CFO should expect that for every dollar approved to build an AI agent, at least one additional dollar will be required in the first twelve months of operations. For agents in regulated industries or high-volume production environments, the ratio is closer to two. Any business case that does not budget operating costs at parity with build costs is structurally underestimating the investment. This is not a precise formula. It is a planning assumption that is closer to reality than the current default, which in most enterprises is zero.

The ratio matters. The 40 to 60 percent TCO underestimation documented by HyperSense Software suggests that the below-waterline costs can exceed the above-waterline costs within the first year of production. The business case modelled the visible half. The invisible half showed up as a budget variance that nobody could attribute to a single cause, because the costs were distributed across infrastructure invoices, contractor hours, and operational overhead that the finance function had no reason to connect to a specific AI agent.

THE BUDGET THAT DOES NOT EXIST

The visibility gap documented in the previous chapter is worth restating briefly, because its financial consequence is the subject of this one. CB Insights found that 40 percent of executives cannot track agent ROI, even as 80 percent rate AI agents a strategic priority. The organisation is accelerating investment in a category where it cannot measure the return.

The structural cause is not negligence. It is that AI operating costs do not fit any existing budget category. They are not infrastructure, because they scale with user behaviour rather than provisioned capacity. They do not resemble headcount costs, because the human oversight expense is embedded within the agent's operating model rather than appearing as a separate payroll line. And unlike software licensing, the cost is consumption-based and variable rather than fixed and annual. Every budgeting template the finance function has ever used was designed for deterministic cost structures where the relationship between input and output cost is stable. AI breaks that relationship.

As one CIO advisor told CIO.com: "We see horror stories where companies sign large contracts, but actual internal adoption is incredibly low." The invoice arrives. The adoption does not match it. The finance team has no framework to reconcile the gap because the gap exists in a cost category that does not have a name in the chart of accounts.

The metrics most enterprises do track make the problem harder to see. Vendor dashboards report productivity gains: hours saved, tasks automated, queries resolved. These are adoption metrics, not economic metrics. They measure the benefit side of the equation without the cost side. An enterprise that reports five hundred hours saved per month has measured what the agent did. It has not measured what the agent cost. The hours saved are real. Whether those hours cost less than the agent that saved them is a question the dashboard was not designed to answer.

The question of how to budget for AI at all is producing some useful partial answers. The most effective CIOs, according to TechTarget's analysis in early 2026, present unit economics that finance teams can pressure-test at each stage: 70 percent of AI spend directed to scaling proven workflows, 20 percent to adjacent expansions, 10 percent to frontier experiments. This portfolio approach treats AI investment the way venture capital treats a fund, with the recognition that not every bet will pay off but every bet must be measurable. TechTarget's distinction between operational efficiency spend (opex) and new revenue infrastructure (capex) gives the finance function at least a starting classification.

But stage-gated budgeting governs allocation. It does not govern operating costs after allocation. The budget was approved. The agents were deployed. The operating costs compound at the task level, and the financial governance model has no mechanism to track cost per task, compare it against the human baseline, or flag the moment the economics invert. That moment has a name.

Negative unit economics: when an AI agent costs more per task than the human process it replaced. It is not a measurement failure. It is a structural consequence of deploying probabilistic systems through financial governance designed for deterministic technology. And in most enterprises, nobody is tracking it.

THE LOSS YOU CANNOT SEE

The instinct, when confronted with the cost of building delivery discipline, is to ask for the return on investment. The question sounds reasonable. It is the wrong question.

The return on delivery discipline is not revenue generated. It is loss avoided. The losses are already occurring. They are occurring in every enterprise that has deployed AI agents without task-level economic visibility, without production-condition testing, without continuous governance. The losses are invisible precisely because the financial governance model was not designed to detect them.

Consider the inverse. Starbucks has operated AI in production for seven years. Deep Brew, their AI platform, is estimated by industry analysts to have delivered a 30 percent return on AI investment by fiscal 2024, with the Rewards programme growing to 33.8 million active members and AI-powered personalisation driving meaningful incremental revenue that Starbucks does not disclose separately. Starbucks did not achieve this by deploying a better model than its competitors. It achieved it through seven years of continuous operational discipline. The returns did not arrive in the first quarter. They arrived after years of building the infrastructure that made the models productive at scale. The discipline preceded the return by years, not months. Chapter 9 examines the Starbucks pattern in detail.

And as Starbucks expanded its AI capabilities, it needed more operational infrastructure, not less. Better models did not reduce the need for governance. Better models increased it. The operational cost grew with capability. Any business case that assumes operational costs decrease as models improve is modelling the wrong cost curve.

The question is not what delivery discipline costs. It is what the absence of delivery discipline costs.

For the enterprises described in the previous chapters, the answer includes regulatory liability when an agent provides incorrect information to customers, customer trust erosion when service quality degrades without detection, budget overruns that compound quarterly because the cost tracking infrastructure does not exist, and AI programmes that consume increasing resources while delivering diminishing returns that nobody can measure. Those costs are real. They are quantifiable after the fact, when the incident arrives and forces the quantification. Delivery discipline makes them visible before the incident arrives. That is the return.

CB Insights framed the strategic consequence precisely: "Investing in measurement infrastructure today will separate successful deployments from costly experiments tomorrow." The gap between strategic intent and economic visibility is not closing. It is widening with every agent deployed into production without task-level cost governance.

THE PRESSURE POINT

Four chapters of diagnosis, and the structural picture is now complete. Enterprise AI pilots succeed and production fails because the delivery system was designed for a different kind of technology. That is a category error, not a competence failure. The category error produces five predictable failure modes that compound across an agent portfolio. And underneath it all, the economics are fundamentally different from anything the enterprise has governed before, with cost structures that the financial model cannot detect and operating expenses that no budget category was built to capture.

The weight of the problem is not theoretical. It is accumulating in real time across every enterprise with AI agents in production.

> *Your AI agents may already cost more per task than the people they replaced. You would not know, because nothing in your financial governance was designed to tell you.*

Agents are drifting without detection. Governance is checking boxes rather than checking systems. Accountability is fragmented across teams that did not ask for it. And the economics are compounding at the task level, invisible to the finance function, because nobody built the instruments to make them visible.

The CFO now has a question that the current operating model cannot answer: what does each agent actually cost per task, and is that cost above or below the human process it replaced? The CIO has a question the current delivery model cannot answer: how do we govern systems that change their own behaviour in production?

The CAIO has a question that no existing framework addresses: what is the operational discipline that sits between deploying AI systems and sustaining them?

Three questions. One structural gap. The delivery discipline that would answer all three does not exist in most organisations. The diagnosis is complete. The discipline starts now.

PART II:
Discipline

The project ends.
The system does not.
That is the gap
no one planned for.

VIJAYAN SEENISAMY

CHAPTER 5

From Project Management to System Stewardship

In early 2026, a team across MIT, Harvard Medical School, and eight other institutions deployed an agentic AI system for cancer surveillance. The system processed hundreds of clinical notes in minutes. It caught adverse events that manual review would have found in days. The technology worked on day one.

It also worked on day thirty. And day sixty. Not because the model improved, but because the team had built something around it: adaptive monitoring that tracked drift in real time, governance that clarified risk at every stage of the agentic process, named accountability at each decision point, and data pipelines engineered for agent compatibility rather than human consumption. The MIT study described in Chapter 2, where eighty percent of the effort went into operating infrastructure, is the pattern system stewardship is designed to replicate.

They did not call what they built system stewardship. But that is what it was.

Most enterprise AI teams never build it. That is why most enterprise AI fails.

The coworker instinct described in Chapter 2, the recognition by three quarters of executives that agents behave more like colleagues than tools, has a practical implication that most enterprises have not yet acted on: if AI agents are coworkers, they need an operating model designed for coworkers, one that governs their ongoing performance, manages their costs, and ensures their outputs remain reliable.

> *Project management is an operating model for building things. System stewardship is an operating model for working alongside things that change.*

The diagnosis is necessary but insufficient. A CIO who understands why the current model fails still needs to know what replaces it. A CFO who recognises the category error still needs to know what to fund instead. A Chief AI Officer who sees the structural gap still needs an operating model to fill it.

The replacement is system stewardship.

The BCG ratio described in Chapter 3, ten percent technology, twenty percent data, seventy percent people and processes, tells you where the replacement discipline must operate. Not in the model layer. Not in the data pipeline. In the operating model: the roles, the governance, the economics, and the accountability structures that determine whether a working AI system produces enterprise outcomes or merely produces outputs that nobody trusts enough to act on.

BCG,
"How Agents Are Accelerating the Next Wave of AI Value Creation," December 2025.

A DIFFERENT SET OF ASSUMPTIONS

System stewardship is the ongoing practice of monitoring, evaluating, governing, and adapting AI systems in production. The distinction from project management is not cosmetic. It reflects a fundamentally different set of assumptions about what the work is.

Project management assumes a defined end state. You plan, build, test, and deploy. The project closes. The team moves on. Success is measured at the point of delivery.

System stewardship assumes a living system. There is no defined end state because the system is never finished. It is always becoming. Deployment is not the finish line. It is the first day of school, not graduation. The system will drift. Its costs will fluctuate. Its outputs will vary. The data it depends on will change. The regulations that apply to it will evolve. Success is not measured at the point of delivery. It is measured continuously, across multiple dimensions, for as long as the system operates.

This is not a subtle distinction. It changes everything about how the work is structured.

Critically, system stewardship is not a post-deployment function bolted onto an existing project. It has two phases, and both are essential. During delivery, the stewardship model itself is designed and built as a core deliverable alongside the AI system: the evaluation cadence, the drift baselines, the cost models, the escalation logic, the accountability structure. In production, that model is operated continuously. If the stewardship infrastructure is not built during delivery, there is nothing to operate in production. The team that inherits the system inherits silence.

Build the stewardship model during delivery or inherit nothing in production. There is no third option.

DIMENSION	PROJECT MANAGEMENT	SYSTEM STEWARDSHIP
Core assumption	The system has a defined end state. Build it, ship it, close the project.	The system is never finished. It is always becoming. Deployment is the beginning of operations, not the end.
Success question	Did we deliver on time, on budget, and to specification?	Is the system healthy, safe, economically viable, and learning?
Accountability	A project manager owns a timeline. The project closes. The team moves on.	A steward owns system health. Accountability persists for as long as the system operates.
Governance	Milestone-based review at defined checkpoints.	Continuous evaluation. The system changes between checkpoints, so checkpoint-based review is structurally insufficient.
Economics	Project budget with a defined return period. Capex profile.	Operating expenditure tracked at the level of individual tasks. Opex profile that must be governed continuously.
Monitoring	Verify at deployment. Hand over to operations.	Permanent operational function. Adaptive, not static. Measures output quality, not just infrastructure health.

The left column describes how every enterprise currently manages technology. The right column describes what AI systems actually require.

FIGURE 5.1
Project Management vs System Stewardship

WHAT THIS CHANGES

The shift from project management to system stewardship is not a process update. It rewires the assumptions underneath four executive functions simultaneously.

The CIO faces a redesign, not a retraining exercise. Adding AI to a project manager's responsibilities does not create stewardship. It creates a project manager with an impossible job: accountable for a system whose behaviour changes after the project closes, using tools and processes that assume the behaviour is stable. The delivery organisation needs new roles, a new accountability model, and a new relationship with production operations that does not end at handover.

The investment model must change with it. AI systems do not have the capital expenditure profile that the CFO's team is accustomed to governing. They have an operating expenditure profile that must be tracked continuously. The business case does not close at go-live. It must be re-evaluated as the system's behaviour and economics change. A system that was cost-effective at deployment may reach negative unit economics three months later if nobody is tracking cost per task.

The Chief AI Officer may recognise this chapter as the operating model she has been looking for. System stewardship is the discipline that connects strategy to operations. It tells leadership what to govern, architecture what to support, and infrastructure what to measure. Without it, each function optimises independently. With it, the organisation has a chance of actually running AI at scale.

And at the board level, it reframes the conversation entirely. The question is not whether to invest in AI. That decision has been made. The question is whether the organisation has built the operational discipline to protect and sustain that investment. System stewardship is the answer to the board member who asks: "We have spent $50 million on AI. What is the governance model for that investment after the projects close?"

WHAT THE DISCIPLINE REQUIRES

System stewardship is not a rebrand of existing project management. The delivery discipline required for enterprise AI is structurally different. It must address requirements that traditional delivery does not, and the absence of any one creates a gap the others cannot compensate for.

The previous three chapters described where the current model breaks. The discipline must address all of it simultaneously: continuous evaluation rather than checkpoint-based testing, because the system changes between checkpoints. Economic governance at the level of individual tasks, not project budgets, because the cost structure is consumption-based and variable. Defined accountability that survives project closure, because the handover point that every delivery methodology assumes does not exist for a probabilistic system. And governance designed for output quality on a spectrum, not binary pass/fail.

Any one of these requirements would be manageable in isolation. The difficulty is that neglecting any single one creates a failure mode the others cannot detect. Continuous evaluation without economic governance catches quality drift while costs silently compound. Task-level economics without persistent accountability tracks the numbers with nobody authorised to act on them.

> *The agent acts. The system evaluates. The human decides. Every step is recorded. That loop is the discipline.*

Scaling protocols that prevent pilot-to-production collapse. Managing one AI agent is a team effort. Managing fifty is a portfolio management discipline with fundamentally different staffing ratios, governance cadences, and observability requirements. Most enterprises design their AI operating model for the single pilot they are running today. When the second agent launches, they duplicate the team. By the fifth agent, they have five bespoke teams with no shared governance, no common evaluation standards, and no portfolio-level visibility into aggregate cost or risk. System stewardship must be designed for the portfolio the enterprise is building toward, not the single use case it started with.

Not every enterprise needs all of these capabilities on day one. The discipline matures in stages. The AI Role Operating Framework™ defines four: Ad-Hoc, where agents are deployed based on demos that worked and nobody owns production. Repeatable, where templates and early risk checks are emerging, but evaluation is inconsistent. Scalable, where policies for drift detection, rollback, and cost governance are in place and a named steward owns reliability. Enterprise Ready, where AI delivery is embedded in enterprise governance with board-level visibility across the full portfolio. Most enterprises believe they are Scalable. Most, when they answer honest questions, discover they are in the upper range of Repeatable. Chapter 11 provides the diagnostic that tells you exactly where you stand.

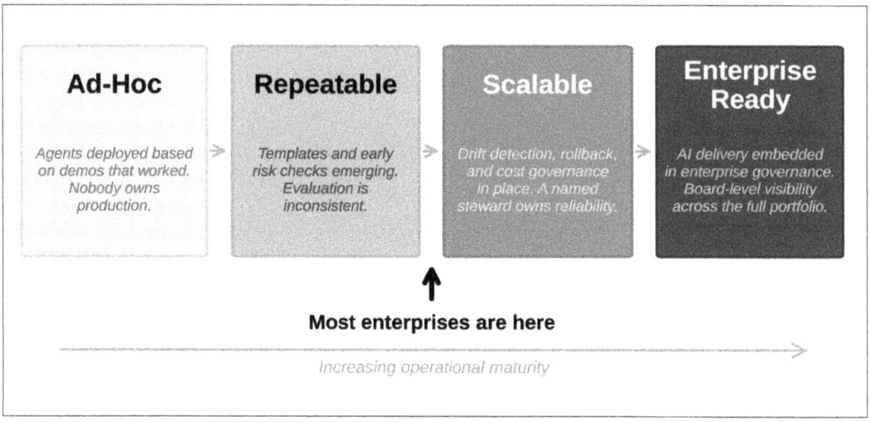

Four stages of system stewardship maturity, from reactive deployment to enterprise-wide governance. The jump from Repeatable to Scalable requires structural capabilities (named stewards, drift detection, cost governance) that cannot be added incrementally. Chapter 11 provides the diagnostic that tells you exactly where you stand.

FIGURE 5.2
The Four Stages of System Stewardship Maturity

SEVEN FRAMEWORKS, ZERO OPERATING MODELS

The need for governance is not unrecognised. By April 2026, at least seven governance frameworks had been published specifically for AI systems: Singapore's Model Governance Framework for Generative AI, the OWASP Agentic AI Top 10, Google's five-layer Responsible AI model, NIST CAISI, the Colorado AI Act enforcement framework, the EU AI Act risk-based approach, and ISO/IEC 42001.

None of them solve the problem this chapter addresses.

These frameworks address what to govern. They define risk classifications, documentation requirements, audit trail standards, and compliance obligations. They are necessary and enterprises should adopt them. But they do not address how to operationalise governance continuously in production. They are compliance oriented. System stewardship is operations oriented. The governance framework tells you that your AI system must be auditable. System stewardship is the operating discipline that produces the audit evidence, continuously, as the system runs.

The governance maturity gap documented in Chapter 3 has a corollary. The same Deloitte research found that the enterprises achieving significantly greater business value were the ones where senior leadership actively shaped AI governance, not those delegating it to technical teams. Governance as a leadership discipline produces outcomes. Governance as a technical afterthought does not.

The shift is already visible among enterprises that are getting results. An enterprise IT leader surveyed by ETR described the transition: "Once we put all those data points on it, the governance became much more fact-based than emotion based. Now we're saying zoom out, define this thing, go in front of the execs, show them the big picture, and tell them what you're going to do."

ETR (ENTERPRISE TECHNOLOGY RESEARCH),
AI Product Series, February 2026.

That description, the shift from small pilots with informal governance to structured, evidence-based, executive-visible governance, is system stewardship emerging organically. The leaders who are getting results are building pieces of this discipline inside their organisations. They are not calling it system stewardship. They do not have a shared framework. But the pattern is consistent: governance moves from reactive to continuous, measurement moves from project-level to task-level, and accountability moves from temporary project teams to permanent operational roles.

THE WAITING PROBLEM

The natural question is whether to build this discipline now or wait for the major consulting firms and analyst houses to codify it. It is a reasonable instinct. McKinsey, BCG, Deloitte, and Accenture have collectively invested billions in AI capabilities. Gartner and Forrester shape enterprise technology strategy for thousands of organisations. If this discipline is as important as this book argues, surely they will define it.

In February 2026, OpenAI announced Frontier Alliances with McKinsey, BCG, Accenture, and Capgemini. The partnerships are multi-year and well-funded. They tell you exactly what the Big Four are focused on: deploying AI agents into enterprise clients. Operating model redesign. Workflow integration. Change management. Strategy.

What none of them have published is a codified discipline for operating probabilistic systems in production. Some run managed services. Some operate AI infrastructure for clients. Individual engagement teams may practise elements of what this book describes. But no firm has published the framework, the maturity model, or the operating methodology that converts those individual practices into a repeatable enterprise discipline. The discipline does not yet exist as a body of knowledge. It exists as pockets of practice inside teams that have learned it through experience and have no mechanism to scale it beyond the engagement they learned it on.

OPENAI FRONTIER ALLIANCES WITH MCKINSEY,
BCG, Accenture, Capgemini, February 2026.

Gartner publishes hype cycles and magic quadrants. They describe markets. They do not codify operational disciplines. Based on typical research cycles, a Gartner-published AI delivery maturity model is estimated at Q4 2026 to Q2 2027. By that time, enterprises that adopted system stewardship in 2026 will have twelve to eighteen months of operational advantage: established governance cadences, calibrated evaluation baselines, trained stewardship teams, and institutional knowledge of how their AI systems actually behave in production. That institutional knowledge cannot be purchased from a consulting firm. It can only be built by operating the discipline. The organisations that will define best practice are the ones building it now, not the ones waiting for someone else to publish it.

WHAT EXISTS AND WHAT DOES NOT

The Chief AI Officer inherits the frustration most directly. A portfolio of AI systems with no operational discipline behind them. The CIO's delivery teams built them as projects and moved on. The infrastructure team monitors uptime but has no visibility into output quality. The governance framework was designed for a different kind of technology. You can see the gap, but when you try to describe what needs to fill it, you find yourself inventing vocabulary because the discipline has not been named yet.

That is the current state, honestly described. This discipline is being invented in real time. No single organisation has fully codified it. The elements described in this chapter, continuous evaluation, task-level economics, persistent accountability, probabilistic governance, portfolio scaling, are visible in fragments across leading enterprises and research institutions. What does not yet exist is a unified operating model that integrates them into a coherent practice.

That is what the remainder of this book provides.

The intellectual foundation is clear. The evidence for why this discipline is needed is overwhelming. The gap between what enterprises are deploying and how they are managing those deployments is widening with every new agent that enters production without an operational discipline behind it. Each month of that widening gap produces systems that drift further from their intended performance, costs that compound without visibility, and governance decisions that are made on the basis of project metrics that no longer describe reality.

The question is no longer whether enterprises need system stewardship. It is whether yours will build it before or after the first production failure that your current operating model cannot explain.

If you cannot name
the control surfaces,
you are not managing the system.
You are watching it run.

VIJAYAN SEENISAMY

CHAPTER 6

The Five Control Surfaces

An aircraft has control surfaces: ailerons, elevators, a rudder. Each gives the pilot a different form of authority over the aircraft's behaviour. Lose one and the aircraft still flies, but the pilot's ability to respond to changing conditions is degraded. Lose two and the margins narrow to the point where an experienced pilot is managing consequences rather than directing outcomes.

AI systems in production have the same structural characteristic. They require multiple, simultaneous forms of control, each governing a different dimension of the system's behaviour. The discipline of system stewardship, described in the previous chapter, operates across five of these control surfaces. Neglect one and the system fails in ways the other four cannot detect.

This chapter defines the structure: five control surfaces, each giving the operator a different form of authority over the system, all five required simultaneously. It does not prescribe specific practices, templates, or cadences. Those are operational decisions that depend on context. What it provides is the structural model: the minimum set of control surfaces required for an enterprise to claim it is managing its AI systems, rather than merely running them.

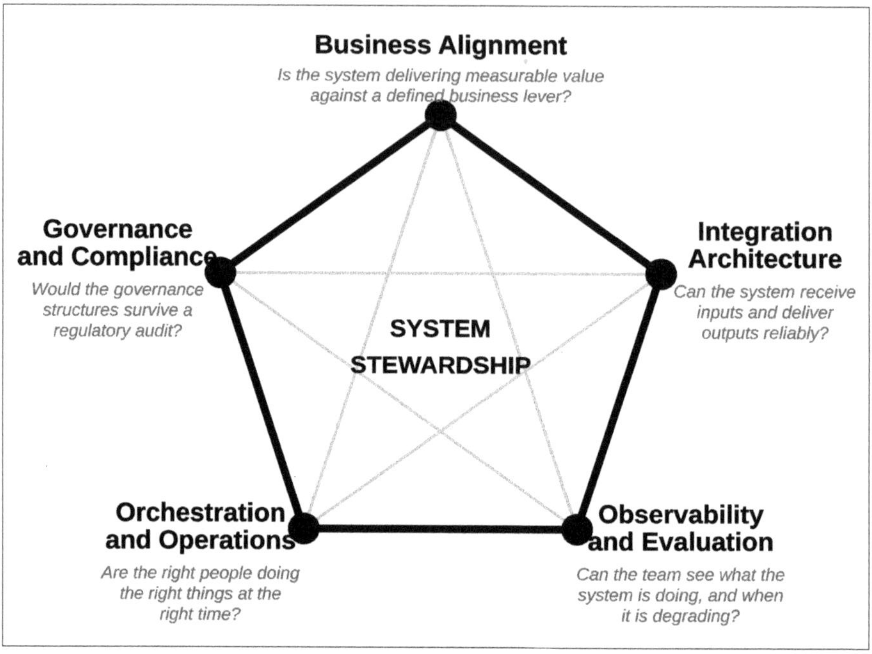

Each surface governs a different dimension of the system. Together, they provide complete operational authority. Individually, they create blind spots.

FIGURE 6.1
The Five Control Surfaces: Pentagon Model

The pentagon is the recurring image of this book. When it appears in later chapters mapped to success patterns, assessment results, and the five-agent test, it represents the same structural claim: all five surfaces must be present. A missing vertex is not a gap. It is a blind spot the other four cannot cover.

BUSINESS ALIGNMENT: WHERE THE SYSTEM IS POINTED

The first control surface governs the relationship between the AI system and the business outcome it was deployed to produce. This sounds obvious. It is not. Most enterprises can articulate why they built the system. Fewer can articulate whether the system, right now, in production, is delivering against that business case.

The problem is not that organisations lack business cases. It is that business cases are written at the start of a project and rarely revisited after deployment. The AI system enters production with a stated purpose. Then the system's behaviour changes, its costs shift, the business context evolves, and nobody recalibrates the alignment between what the system is doing and what the business needs it to do.

CB Insights found that 40% of enterprises cannot track ROI on their AI agents. This is not a measurement problem. It is a structural one. The business case was built for the project. When the project closed, the measurement framework closed with it. The system is still running. The business case is not.

CB INSIGHTS,
AI Agent ROI Executive Survey, Q4 2025.

Business alignment as a control surface means maintaining continuous visibility into whether the system is producing the value it was deployed to produce, whether the economics still support that value, and whether the business context has changed in ways that require the system to be redirected. Without this surface, an enterprise can operate a technically sound AI system that produces outcomes nobody needs.

INTEGRATION ARCHITECTURE: THE STRUCTURAL INTEGRITY

Integration architecture governs how the AI system connects to everything around it: data sources, APIs, downstream workflows, enterprise systems, and other agents. This is the surface most enterprises manage reasonably well, because it maps to existing engineering disciplines. CI/CD pipelines exist. API gateways exist. Infrastructure monitoring exists.

What does not exist, in most cases, is integration governance designed for systems whose outputs vary on a spectrum. A pipeline that reliably delivers unreliable outputs is not a functioning integration. It is a transmission mechanism for degraded quality. Integration testing for AI systems must verify not just connectivity but output quality across the integration boundary, and that distinction changes what the integration architecture must be designed to detect.

Integration architecture also governs rollback capability, which is structurally different for AI systems. Rolling back a deterministic software release means deploying the previous version. Rolling back an AI agent is more complex: the model may have been updated, the prompts may have changed, the context window may reference data that has shifted. The rollback path must be defined and tested before deployment, not improvised during a production incident.

As the agent portfolio grows, integration architecture must also address multi-agent dependency mapping. When agents depend on other agents, a failure in one can cascade in ways that no single-agent monitoring would detect. The integration surface must maintain a current map of which systems depend on which agents and what happens when an agent degrades or is taken offline.

Starbucks illustrates the complexity of getting this right. Since 2019, Starbucks has operated AI in production across personalisation, inventory, staffing, and store operations, connecting systems through Databricks for ML workflows, MLflow for model tracking, and Datadog and PagerDuty for system health monitoring. What makes their integration work is not the sophistication of the tools. It is the operational discipline that ensures the tools are connected, monitored, and governed as a single system rather than as independent technical capabilities. That cross-functional integration discipline is precisely what most enterprises skip.

The infrastructure underneath makes this harder than most enterprises realise. ADAPT's research across Australian CIOs found that only 47% of key business processes operate in real time, only 50% of employees have access to trusted real-time data to do their jobs, and 40% of mission-critical applications still depend on legacy platforms. These are not AI statistics. They are the infrastructure statistics that determine whether AI integration can work at all. An agent that requires real-time data to make decisions cannot function reliably when half the data it depends on is not available in real time. An integration architecture built on top of legacy dependencies that were designed for batch processing will produce latency, inconsistency, and failure modes that no amount of AI engineering can compensate for. The integration surface is not just about connecting the AI system. It is about whether the enterprise infrastructure underneath can support what the AI system needs to operate continuously.

ADAPT,
CIO Edge Research, 2025.

GOVERNANCE AND COMPLIANCE: THE OPERATING ENVELOPE

Ask a compliance officer whether their organisation's AI governance would survive a regulatory audit. In most enterprises, the honest answer is uncomfortable. IBM's 2025 Cost of a Data Breach Report found that among the 13% of organisations that experienced an AI-related security breach, 97% lacked proper AI access controls. Across all breached organisations, 63% lacked AI governance policies entirely. The systems were in production. The governance was not.

IBM,
Cost of a Data Breach Report, 2025.

Governance defines the boundaries within which the system is permitted to operate. For deterministic systems, the question is whether the system conforms to specification. For AI systems, the question is harder: is the system operating within an acceptable range of behaviour, and does the organisation have the mechanisms to detect when it moves outside that range?

This control surface covers risk classification, which determines how much governance scrutiny an agent receives based on the consequence of failure. A customer-facing financial advice agent and an internal meeting summariser should not operate under the same governance regime. Without risk classification, enterprises apply uniform governance to all agents, which means either over-governing the low-risk ones or under-governing the high-risk ones. Both outcomes waste organisational capacity.

It covers audit trail completeness, because regulatory frameworks now require the ability to demonstrate what the system did, why, and who was accountable. It covers escalation pathways, because probabilistic systems produce edge cases that require human judgement, and those escalation paths must be defined before the edge case arrives. And it covers review cadence, the rhythm at which governance actively evaluates system behaviour rather than waiting for something to go wrong.

The data on this is unambiguous. Four out of five enterprises have no mature governance model for autonomous AI agents. They are governing the most unpredictable technology they have ever deployed with frameworks designed for something else entirely. Governance is not overhead. It is the mechanism through which the enterprise maintains authority over systems that make decisions autonomously.

OBSERVABILITY AND EVALUATION: THE INSTRUMENT PANEL

Can your team tell you, right now, whether your production AI agent is performing better or worse than it was last month? Not whether it is running. Whether it is performing.

That question separates observability from monitoring. Most enterprises believe they already have observability because they have dashboards, logging, and uptime alerts. What they lack, in the majority of cases, is observability designed for probabilistic output quality.

The observability gap documented in Chapter 3 is the defining problem for this surface. Most enterprises have the tooling. The majority do not run systematic evaluations. Observability without evaluation is an instrument panel that nobody reads.

Traditional infrastructure monitoring answers one question: is the system up? Observability for AI systems must answer five distinct questions simultaneously, each tracking a different signal. Quality: is the output accurate and useful? Drift: is performance moving away from established baselines? Economics: are the costs sustainable at the current task volume? Safety: is the system operating within its defined boundaries? Adoption: are the humans who depend on the system actually using it as designed, and are they overriding its outputs in ways that indicate a trust problem?

Each of these questions requires different instrumentation, different baselines, and different response protocols. A system can be technically operational, producing outputs within latency thresholds, consuming resources within budget, and still be generating responses that are subtly wrong in ways that infrastructure metrics will never detect. Drift in output quality is the defining risk of probabilistic systems. If the observability surface does not measure it, the enterprise is flying on instruments that do not show altitude.

ORCHESTRATION AND OPERATIONS: THE THROTTLE AND RUDDER

Where the other four surfaces describe what must be governed, orchestration describes how. It is the coordination discipline that ensures someone receives the signals observability generates, interprets them through the governance framework, evaluates them against business alignment, and acts through the integration architecture. Without orchestration, the other four surfaces produce information that nobody synthesises.

In most enterprises today, orchestration for AI systems does not exist as a formal practice. The engineering team that built the system watches it informally. The business team that funded it checks in periodically. Nobody owns the system's health as a continuous operational responsibility. When something goes wrong, the response is ad hoc: whoever notices the problem first becomes the owner by default. This is not orchestration. It is firefighting.

The consequences are predictable and consistent. Without orchestration, enterprises discover that the same production agent has no named owner, no evaluation cadence, and no defined escalation path. A CAIO becomes the single point of failure for an entire portfolio of agents because nobody else has the authority or the context to make decisions about them. Prompt updates are made without governance review, without testing, and without communication to the teams that depend on the agent's outputs. The ungoverned prompt update pattern described in Chapter 3, where accuracy degraded over a quarter without the team detecting it, is the operational consequence of missing orchestration.

Orchestration as a control surface requires defined role clarity for production AI systems, not just project teams. It requires a delivery rhythm, the cadence at which the system's health is reviewed, its performance evaluated, and its direction confirmed. It requires an evaluation loop that connects what the observability surface detects to what the governance surface permits to what the business alignment surface requires. And it requires an escalation architecture that defines who decides what when the system's behaviour moves outside acceptable parameters.

Orchestration is the connective tissue between the other four surfaces. The role architecture described in Chapter 7 maps specific accountability to this surface, with the AI Delivery Manager owning the coordination rhythm and the AgentOps Lead contributing operational execution. Without it, the enterprise has four independent functions that optimise in isolation while the system as a whole degrades.

THE INTERACTION PROBLEM

The most common mistake in enterprise AI governance is treating these five surfaces as independent capabilities that can be built sequentially. An enterprise might invest in observability tooling (surface four) without establishing the governance framework (surface three) that defines what the observations mean. It might build governance policies (surface three) without the orchestration discipline (surface five) that ensures someone acts on them. Each surface in isolation creates the appearance of control without the substance of it.

The surfaces interact in ways that are not immediately obvious. Consider a scenario that is already common: an AI agent in production begins producing outputs that are subtly less accurate than its baseline. If observability is functioning, this drift is detected. But detection is not resolution. The governance surface must determine whether the drift exceeds the acceptable range. The business alignment surface must assess whether the drift affects the business outcome. The integration surface must determine whether the drift originates in the model, the data pipeline, or an upstream system change. The orchestration surface must coordinate the response across these functions. Remove any one surface from that sequence and the enterprise either misses the drift, misinterprets it, or detects it and fails to respond.

This is why the chapter opened with the aviation metaphor. A pilot does not manage ailerons independently of the rudder. The control surfaces operate as a system. An enterprise that manages governance without observability is applying rules it cannot verify. An enterprise that manages observability without orchestration is generating signals that nobody acts on. An enterprise that manages business alignment without governance is optimising for outcomes it cannot sustain.

> *Most enterprises are managing two control surfaces and calling it governance. The other three are where the failures start.*

WHO PAYS FOR WHAT

One reason these five surfaces are managed inconsistently is that they map to different budget owners. Business alignment sits with the CFO and business units. Integration sits with the CTO. Governance sits with legal, risk, and the CAIO. Observability is split between the CTO and the CAIO. Orchestration, if it is funded at all, sits with the CAIO or a nascent AI delivery function.

This fragmentation is not accidental. It reflects how enterprises have always funded technology: infrastructure to the CTO, compliance to legal, business value to the business. The problem is that AI systems do not respect these organisational boundaries. A governance failure becomes a business alignment problem when it reaches a customer. An observability gap becomes a compliance problem when the auditor asks for evidence. An integration failure becomes an economics problem when retries drive token costs beyond the business case.

CONTROL SURFACE	PRIMARY BUDGET OWNER	WHAT GETS FUNDED
Business Alignment	CFO / Business Unit	Business case reviews, value realisation tracking, ROI governance
Integration Architecture	CTO / Head of Engineering	Infrastructure, API management, deployment pipelines, data engineering
Governance and Compliance	General Counsel / CRO / CAIO	Compliance, audit, risk classification, ethical review
Observability and Evaluation	CTO / CAIO (shared)	Monitoring platforms, drift detection tooling, evaluation infrastructure
Orchestration and Operations	CAIO / AI Delivery Manager	Cross-role coordination, delivery cadence, agent coaching, escalation

The budget owners are different. The system they are funding is the same. Coordination is not optional.

FIGURE 6.2
Control Surface Budget Mapping

The practical implication for the CIO and CAIO is that system stewardship requires a coordination mechanism that operates across these budget boundaries. This does not mean consolidating all AI spending under a single function. It means establishing a shared view of system health that each function contributes to, and each can act on.

FROM STRUCTURE TO PRACTICE

The structural model is intentional. The specific practices depend on context. What does not vary is the minimum set of surfaces. An enterprise may implement them with different tools, different cadences, different organisational structures. But an enterprise that neglects any one of these five surfaces is operating its AI systems with a blind spot that the other four surfaces cannot compensate for. The instrument panel does not replace the rudder. The operating envelope does not replace the ability to see where the aircraft is pointing.

The org chart has no role for
the person who keeps
the AI system alive after
the project team moves on.

VIJAYAN SEENISAMY

CHAPTER 7

The Roles That Do Not Exist Yet

In early 2025, five hundred and twenty-five open positions on LinkedIn with "AI Delivery Manager" in the title. Two years ago, the role did not exist. It still does not have an agreed job description. Salary ranges span from forty-eight thousand dollars to four hundred and twelve thousand, an eightfold spread that tells you nobody has settled on what this person is supposed to do, how senior they should be, or what authority they carry.

That spread is not a recruitment problem. It is a signal. The market is inventing roles faster than it can define them, because the systems described in the previous six chapters require human accountability that no existing role was designed to provide.

Most enterprises are managing two of the five control surfaces, typically integration and some form of observability, because those map to engineering disciplines that predate AI. The other three require accountability structures that do not exist in the current organisational chart.

The question is not whether enterprises need new roles. The market has already answered that. The question is what those roles must govern, how they differ structurally from the roles they are replacing, and why renaming existing positions does not close the gap.

THE STRUCTURAL MISMATCH

Every enterprise role involved in technology delivery was designed for deterministic systems. Project managers track scope, schedule, and budget against a fixed baseline. Scrum masters facilitate ceremonies within a methodology built for predictable iteration cycles. DevOps engineers manage deployment pipelines for software that behaves identically every time it runs. These roles work because the systems they govern are stable after deployment. The project manager hands over to business-as-usual. The delivery team disbands. Accountability transfers to operations, where the system runs until the next release.

Even where enterprises have adopted a 'build it, run it' model and the team stays with the system, the operational practices they use in production were designed for deterministic systems. They monitor infrastructure health, not output quality. They respond to incidents, not to gradual drift. AI systems require continuous delivery-grade attention throughout their production lifecycle, and the operational instruments these teams rely on were not designed to provide it.

The levels of autonomy, complexity, and risk these systems introduce demand more than new titles. They demand new accountability structures. An enterprise that assigns a deterministic role to manage a probabilistic system has not solved the staffing problem. It has embedded the category error into the organisational chart.

This is why the 525 positions exist with an eightfold salary spread. Enterprises know they need someone in this seat. They do not yet know what the seat requires, because they are defining it against the wrong reference point. They are writing job descriptions for deterministic delivery managers and adding the word "AI" to the title. The title changed. The accountability model did not.

> *Five hundred and twenty-five open roles. An eightfold salary spread. The market is hiring for a role it has not yet defined. That is not a talent shortage. It is a design failure.*

THE ROLE ARCHITECTURE

System stewardship, the discipline described in Chapter 5, requires four distinct roles. Each occupies a different quadrant of the operating model, defined by two axes: organisational accountability versus technical accountability, and system design versus system operations. Together with a foundational engineering capacity, they form the minimum role architecture for an enterprise managing AI systems in production.

These are not new titles applied to old jobs. Each represents a structural shift in what the enterprise expects the role to govern and how long that accountability lasts.

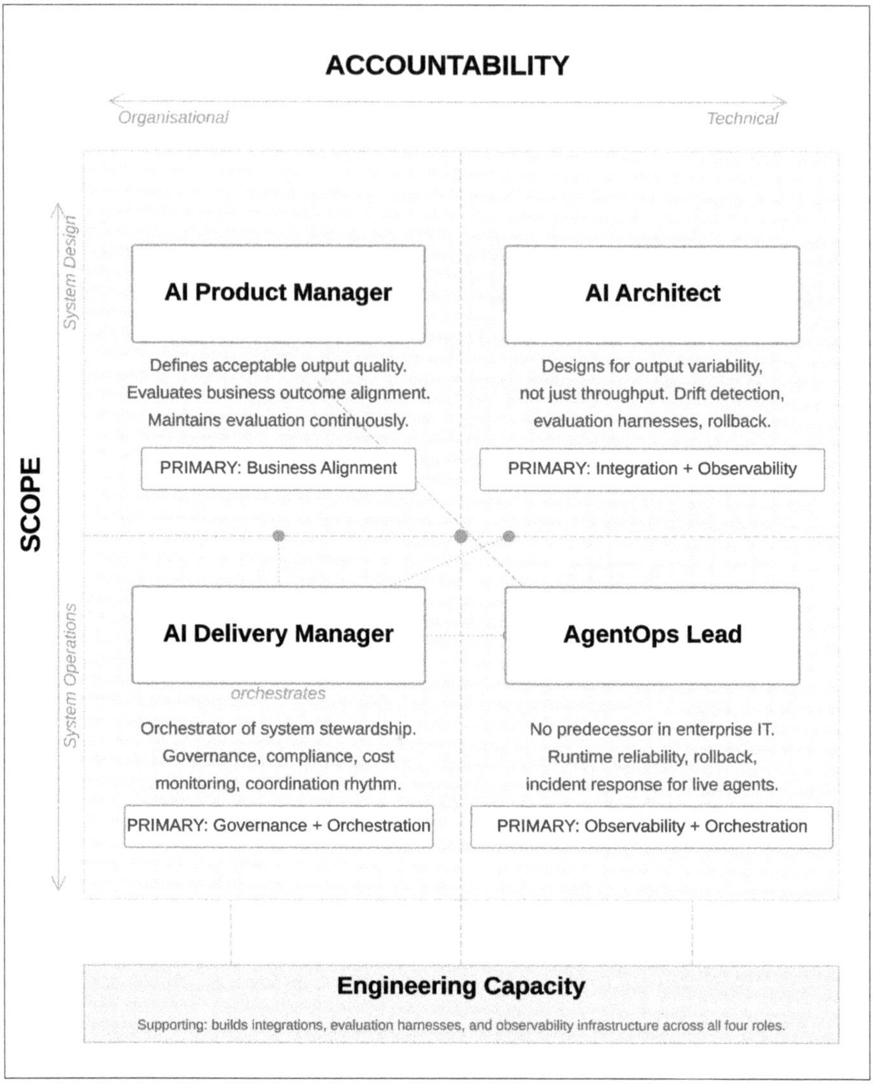

Four roles occupy distinct quadrants defined by accountability type and operational scope. Dashed lines show the AI Delivery Manager's orchestration function connecting the other three roles. Engineering capacity supports all four as foundational infrastructure.

FIGURE 7.1
The Role Architecture for System Stewardship

The AI Architect operates at the intersection of technical accountability and system design. In deterministic systems, the architect designs for predictable behaviour at scale. In probabilistic systems, the architect must design for output variability, not just throughput. This means drift detection built into the architecture, evaluation harnesses that test output quality rather than system availability, and rollback capability that accounts for the fact that rolling back an AI agent is structurally different from rolling back a software release. The AI Architect governs the integration architecture and observability control surfaces at the design level, ensuring the system is built to be monitored, not just built to run.

The AI Product Manager operates at the intersection of organisational accountability and system design. The shift here is from managing features to managing behaviour. A traditional product manager defines requirements, prioritises a backlog, and measures adoption. An AI Product Manager defines acceptable output quality, evaluates whether the system's behaviour aligns with the business outcome it was deployed to serve, and maintains that evaluation continuously rather than closing it at launch. This role governs the business alignment control surface. It owns the question that Chapter 6 identified as the one most enterprises stop asking after deployment: is this system still delivering measurable value against a defined business lever? The quality thresholds this role defines feed directly into the governance envelope, making the AI Product Manager a contributing voice in governance decisions even though the governance surface itself is owned elsewhere.

The AI Delivery Manager operates at the intersection of organisational accountability and system operations. This is the orchestrator of system stewardship. Where traditional delivery managers coordinate project teams and hand over to operations at go-live, the AI Delivery Manager's accountability begins during delivery, where the stewardship model is built, and extends through the production lifecycle. The role governs orchestration and operations, the control surface that Chapter 6 identified as the connective tissue between the other four. It owns governance enforcement, compliance evidence, cost monitoring, and the coordination rhythm that ensures the other roles are acting on what the observability surface detects. In the budget mapping from the previous chapter, this role sits in the line item that most enterprises have not created yet: the orchestration function that connects the CTO's infrastructure, the CFO's business case, the General Counsel's compliance framework, and the CAIO's AI strategy into a single operating cadence.

The AgentOps Lead operates at the intersection of technical accountability and system operations. This is the only role in the architecture with no direct predecessor in enterprise technology. The other roles each map onto an established foundation. Delivery management, architecture, and product management each have decades of practice behind them. The AgentOps Lead adapted nothing because the function it governs did not exist before agentic AI. Operations teams were built for deterministic systems. Managing live autonomous agents, where behaviour drifts, outputs degrade unpredictably, and rollback is structurally different from reverting a software release, had no established function and therefore no established role. This role stabilises live agent operations, manages runtime reliability, executes rollback when agents degrade, and runs the incident response protocols those teams were never designed to handle. It governs the observability surface and operates the orchestration infrastructure at the technical layer, the only role in this architecture whose entire accountability sits below the business logic, in the layer where the system either holds or fails.

Engineering capacity remains foundational but no longer carries the system alone. Previously, engineering built, deployed, and often managed the system end to end. In the stewardship model, engineering supports all four roles as part of a wider accountability structure. The engineers build the integrations, evaluation harnesses, and observability infrastructure. They do not own the governance, business alignment, or coaching decisions. That separation of concerns is what distinguishes a stewardship model from a delivery model that happens to include AI.

The architecture describes four accountabilities, not necessarily four headcounts. In an enterprise with a mature AI portfolio, each role may be a dedicated position. In a smaller organisation or an early-stage programme, the same accountabilities may sit with existing leaders. A product manager absorbs business alignment. An SRE lead absorbs AgentOps. A delivery lead absorbs orchestration and governance. What cannot be compressed is the accountability itself. An enterprise that assigns all five control surfaces to a single person has not adopted the model. It has renamed the problem. The structure scales. The accountability does not.

ROLE	BUSINESS ALIGNMENT	INTEGRATION ARCHITECTURE	GOVERNANCE & COMPLIANCE	OBSERVABILITY & EVALUATION	ORCHESTRATION & OPERATIONS
AI Architect		Primary		Primary	
AI Product Manager	Primary		Contributing		
AI Delivery Manager	Contributing		Primary	Contributing	Primary
AgentOps Lead		Contributing	Contributing	Primary	Contributing
Engineering Capacity		Supporting		Supporting	Supporting

Primary = accountable for this surface. Contributing = active role in surface operations. Supporting = builds infrastructure that the surface depends on. Blank = no direct accountability.

FIGURE 7.2
Role-to-Control-Surface Accountability Map

The table makes visible what most enterprises have not mapped. In a typical organisation, the AI Architect and engineering team share accountability for integration and observability. Nobody owns business alignment after the project closes. Nobody owns governance in an operational cadence. Nobody owns orchestration at all. The three empty columns are the three control surfaces that Chapter 6 identified as the ones most enterprises have not built. They are empty because the roles that would fill them do not yet exist in the organisational chart.

FROM ROLES TO OPERATING SYSTEM

Four roles are necessary but not sufficient. The five control surfaces define what the enterprise must govern. The four dimensions that follow define how. A role without an operating rhythm is a title on a business card. The roles described above function within a wider operating system structured around four dimensions: people, processes, platforms, and performance.

The people dimension is the one this chapter has described: the stewards who own reliability, compliance, and business alignment through ongoing attention, not one-time configuration. The AI Product Manager owns customer safety. The AgentOps Lead owns runtime reliability. The AI Delivery Manager owns governance evidence. These are permanent accountabilities, not project assignments.

The process dimension defines the rhythms these roles operate within. Evaluation loops that are frequent, lightweight, and calibrated to risk. Escalation pathways with a single owner per class of risk, not a committee. Release gates based on evidence, not opinion. The cadence is different from project delivery because the system does not have a release date. It has a continuous production lifecycle that requires regular, structured attention at intervals the enterprise defines based on the risk profile of each agent.

The platform dimension provides the technical spine. Observability infrastructure for drift, grounding, and latency. Cost and usage guardrails with defined caps and, where the risk warrants it, automated kill switches. Compliance logging with replayable traces that produce the audit evidence regulators will require. These platforms exist in some enterprises already. What does not exist is the integration between the platforms and the role architecture that acts on what the platforms detect.

The performance dimension defines the signals. Reliability tracked as task success rate by scenario, not as system uptime. Safety tracked as policy violation rate. Economics tracked as cost per successful outcome, the metric that Chapter 4 identified as the one most enterprises cannot currently calculate. These signals connect the observability surface to the business alignment surface through a shared measurement framework that every role in the architecture can read.

The four dimensions interact. A role without a defined process has accountability but no rhythm. A process without platform support has a cadence but no signals. A platform without performance metrics has data but no meaning. The operating system works when all four dimensions are present and connected. It fails, predictably and silently, when any one is missing.

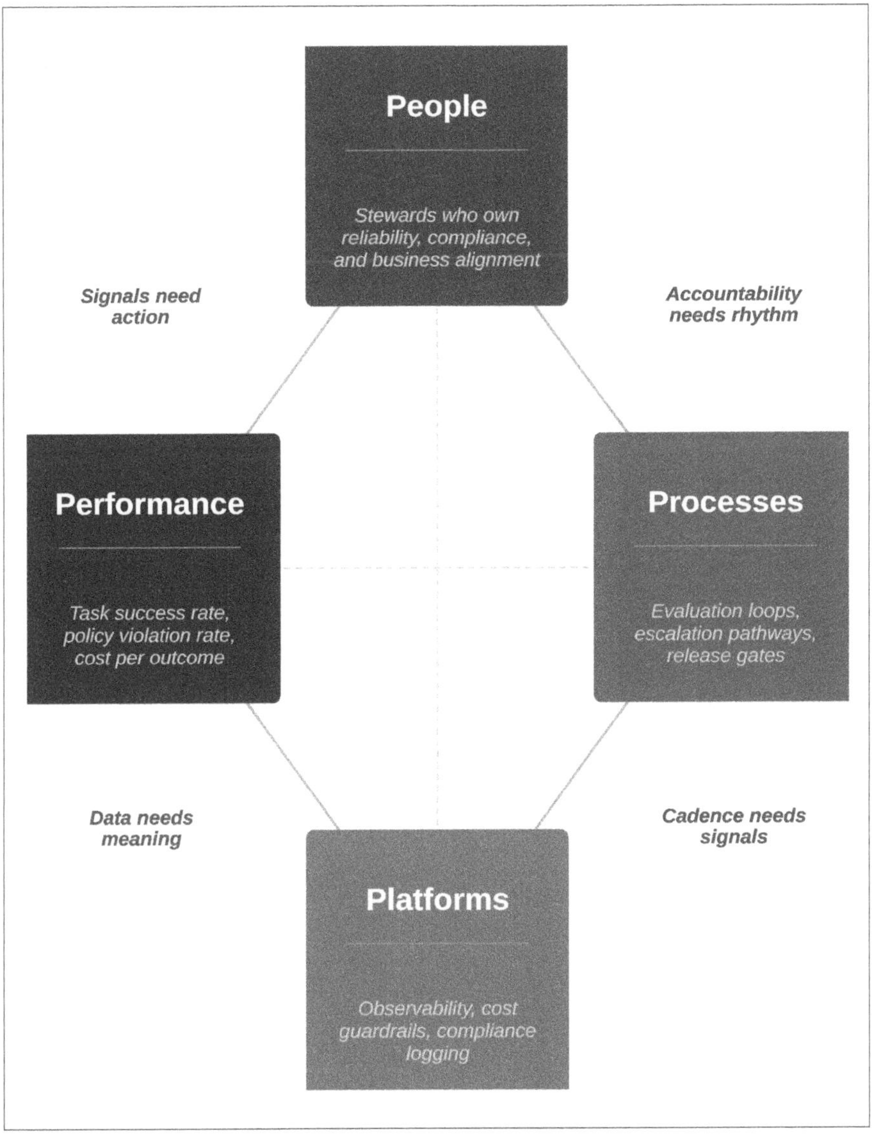

Roles without processes have accountability but no rhythm. Processes without platforms have cadence but no signals. Platforms without performance metrics have data but no meaning. All four dimensions must be present and connected.

FIGURE 7.3
The Four Dimensions of the Operating System

THE GAP IN THE ORGANISATIONAL CHART

The honest assessment for most enterprises is that they have fragments of this architecture, not the architecture itself. An architect who occasionally reviews agent outputs, but whose formal accountability ended at deployment. A product manager who built the business case but transferred ownership to a business unit that has no mechanism for tracking whether the system still delivers against it. An operations team that monitors infrastructure health without monitoring agent behaviour. An AI programme lead whose title includes the word "delivery" but whose mandate, budget profile, and evaluation cadence are identical to the project manager they replaced.

The fragments create a dangerous illusion. The enterprise believes roles are in place because people are assigned to the work. But the accountability model those people operate within was designed for deterministic systems. They are doing their best inside a structure that cannot support what the system requires. The failure described in Chapter 3, fragmented accountability, is not a people problem. It is an architectural one. The people are capable. The roles are not.

Most enterprises have tried to solve this problem before. The pattern is familiar: a centralised Centre of Excellence is established, staffed with specialists, and given a mandate to govern AI across the organisation. In practice, one of two patterns emerges.

Either the CoE becomes a bottleneck that business units route around, creating shadow AI operations with no governance at all, or the CoE is dismantled in a reorganisation and accountability disperses back to individual teams who lack the specialist capability the CoE was created to provide. The enterprise oscillates between centralised control that cannot keep pace and distributed chaos that cannot maintain standards. The role architecture described in this chapter is designed to break that cycle. It distributes accountability to the people closest to the systems while connecting them through shared surfaces, shared signals, and a shared operating cadence. The discipline is neither centralised nor distributed. It is federated: local accountability within an enterprise-wide operating model.

> *You do not solve a structural mismatch by asking better people to work harder inside the wrong structure. You redesign the structure.*

The coworker instinct has a practical consequence. Coworkers who make autonomous decisions in a changing environment need a management architecture designed for that reality. The architecture described here, four roles mapped to five control surfaces within an operating system of people, processes, platforms, and performance, is that design. Knowing who stewards the system is necessary. It is not sufficient. The next question is how.

You do not train
a probabilistic system once
and walk away.
You coach it continuously,
or you watch it drift.

VIJAYAN SEENISAMY

CHAPTER 8

Agent Coaching, Not Agent Training

When MIT Sloan Management Review and BCG asked an investment executive how enterprises should manage their AI agents, the answer was revealing. Agents, the executive said, should be "treated like coworkers who need to be trained, coached, supervised."

The word is "trained."

The executive was not selling a framework. Speaking in a research context rather than a boardroom, the executive independently arrived at the language this book has been building toward across the previous seven chapters. The instinct is correct. The vocabulary is almost correct. But there is a word in that sentence that is not enough on its own, and the fact that it sits alongside the right word is precisely the problem this chapter addresses.

The enterprise defaults to training because training is the model it knows. You train employees. You train systems. You define the curriculum, deliver the knowledge, confirm the transfer, and move on. The entire model assumes that once the knowledge is transferred, the recipient operates with that knowledge until the next training cycle. For thirty years of enterprise software, that assumption held. A system trained on Monday operated the same way on Friday. The environment was stable. The outputs were deterministic. Training was sufficient because the system did not change between sessions.

Agentic AI broke that assumption. The enterprise has not noticed yet because the language has not caught up with the reality. When a CAIO says "we need to train our agents," nobody in the room questions the verb. It sounds right. It is wrong. And because the verb is wrong, the operating model built around it inherits the error: it assumes the wrong duration, funds the wrong budget profile, and measures the wrong success metrics.

The coworker instinct has a practical implication that almost no enterprise has acted on. If these systems are coworkers, they need the management practice designed for coworkers who operate in complex, shifting environments. That practice is not training. It is coaching.

> *"Treated like coworkers who need to be trained, coached, supervised."*
>
> **VIBHOR RASTOGI,**
> head of AI and APAC investments, Citi Ventures. MIT Sloan Management Review / BCG, "The Emerging Agentic Enterprise: How Leaders Must Navigate a New Age of AI," November 2025.

WHY TRAINING IS NOT ENOUGH

The training model operates on a sequence that every enterprise recognises: define the curriculum, deliver the knowledge, test the retention, certify the completion, hand over to operations. The model works when two conditions hold. First, the knowledge is stable. Second, the recipient's behaviour after training is predictable from the training itself. Both conditions hold for deterministic systems. Neither holds for probabilistic ones.

An AI agent operating in production on Monday may produce measurably different outputs by Friday. Not because the training failed. Because the data environment shifted, the user behaviour changed, or the upstream systems feeding the agent delivered different patterns. The agent's behaviour is a function of its current operating context, not only of its original configuration. Training addresses the configuration. It does not address the context.

Franziska Weindauer, who leads TÜV AI.Lab, captured the structural problem precisely: "These systems make decisions on their own, and those decisions can directly impact people, workflows, and critical decisions." When the system makes autonomous decisions, the one-time training event is structurally insufficient. The system's decisions on Wednesday are informed by conditions that did not exist during Monday's training. Training assumes the world is stable between sessions. The world is not stable. The agent operates in it anyway.

> *"These systems make decisions on their own, and those decisions can directly impact people, workflows, and critical decisions."*

MIT SLOAN MANAGEMENT REVIEW,
"Agentic AI at Scale: Redefining Management for a Superhuman Workforce," 2025.

The enterprise response to this problem is predictable: retrain more frequently. Quarterly retraining cycles. Monthly model updates. The logic seems sound. If the environment changes, update the training to match. But retraining on a schedule is still training. It assumes the system is stable between sessions. It assumes that the cadence the enterprise selected, quarterly, monthly, weekly, matches the rate of environmental change. It rarely does. The environment changes continuously. The retraining happens periodically. The gap between the two is where production failures live.

You do not train a system that changes its own behaviour in response to a changing environment. You coach it. The distinction is not semantic. It is structural, and it changes how the enterprise budgets, staffs, and governs its AI systems in production.

WHAT COACHING MEANS OPERATIONALLY

Training is a finite event. Coaching is a continuous practice. That single distinction changes the staffing model, the cost structure, and the success metrics for every AI system in production.

Where training transfers knowledge before deployment and measures success by completion, coaching calibrates performance after deployment and measures success by whether the agent is still producing the business result it was deployed to serve. The training model assumes a stable system. The coaching model assumes the opposite: the system's behaviour will change continuously, and the operating model must include feedback loops designed to detect and respond to that change. Figure 8.1 maps the contrast across seven dimensions. It is the slide the CAIO puts in front of the CFO.

DIMENSION	TRAINING MODEL	COACHING MODEL
Duration	Finite event	Continuous practice
Trigger	Pre-deployment	Post-deployment (ongoing)
Focus	Knowledge transfer	Performance calibration
Success Measure	Completion / pass rate	Business outcome alignment
Assumes	System is stable after deployment	System behaviour changes continuously
Budget Treatment	Capex (one-time)	Opex (permanent)
Failure Mode	Obsolescence (trained knowledge decays)	Drift undetected (coaching gaps compound)

This visual gives the CAIO a one-page argument for why coaching is budgeted differently from training. It is the slide they put in front of the CFO.

FIGURE 8.1
Agent Training vs Agent Coaching

BCG's research on enterprise AI deployment surfaced the tension that makes coaching necessary and difficult simultaneously. Excessive supervision negates the autonomy benefits that justified the agent's deployment in the first place. Insufficient oversight creates operational, compliance, and reputational risks that can exceed the value the agent was intended to produce. The calibration problem is real: too much control and you have an expensive system that requires a human for every decision, eliminating the economic case for the agent. Too little control and you have an autonomous system making decisions that nobody is evaluating against business outcomes or safety boundaries.

> *"Excessive supervision negates autonomy benefits. Insufficient oversight creates operational, compliance, and reputational risks."*
>
> **MIT SLOAN MANAGEMENT REVIEW / BCG,**
> "The Emerging Agentic Enterprise: How Leaders Must Navigate a New Age of AI," November 2025.

Coaching is the discipline of finding and maintaining the dynamic equilibrium between those two failure modes. Not a fixed setting determined at deployment and left unchanged. A continuous adjustment based on the agent's observed behaviour, the business context it operates in, and the risk tolerance the enterprise has defined for its outputs. MIT and BCG described the requirement precisely: enterprises need "dynamic, risk-based oversight mechanisms." Dynamic, meaning they change as conditions change. Risk-based, meaning the intensity of oversight is calibrated to the consequence of getting it wrong, not applied uniformly across every agent in the portfolio.

Operationally, coaching involves interpreting the signals that the observability surface generates, evaluating those signals against the governance framework and business alignment requirements, and calibrating the agent's operating parameters in response. When a monitoring dashboard shows that an agent's accuracy has drifted three points below baseline, training would prescribe a retraining cycle on a schedule. Coaching asks: what caused the drift, is it within acceptable variance for this business context, does the risk profile require immediate intervention or continued observation, and what is the minimum adjustment that restores alignment without over-correcting? The difference is not speed. It is judgement applied continuously rather than procedure applied periodically.

This is why coaching requires the five control surfaces described in Chapter 6 to operate simultaneously. The observability surface detects the signal. The governance surface defines the acceptable range. The business alignment surface determines whether the drift matters to the outcome the agent was deployed to serve. The integration surface enables the technical response. The orchestration surface ensures someone with the authority and the context actually makes the decision. Coaching is the practice that connects these surfaces at the level of the individual agent. Without it, the surfaces generate information. With it, the information becomes action.

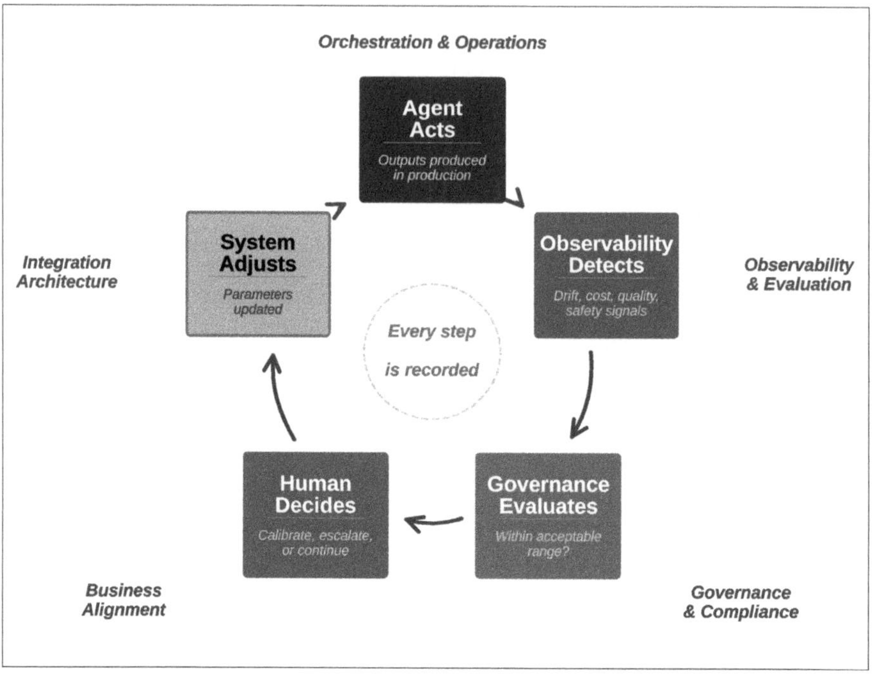

The operational rhythm of agent coaching. Each stage maps to a control surface from Chapter 6. The loop is continuous because the system never reaches a stable state. Every step produces a record.

FIGURE 8.2
The Coaching Loop

THE BUDGET IMPLICATION

The training-coaching distinction has a direct financial consequence that the CFO's team needs to understand before the next budget cycle. Training is a one-time cost. It fits naturally into a capital expenditure profile: invest in the setup, amortise the cost, move on. Coaching is an ongoing operational expense. It does not amortise. It persists for as long as the agent operates, because the agent's behaviour never reaches a stable state that requires no further attention.

When the enterprise budgets AI as a project with a training line item, it structurally underfunds the operational practice that production agents require. The project closes. The budget closes with it. The agent continues operating. Nobody has the mandate or the funding to coach it, because coaching was never a line item. The invisible operating cost described in Chapter 4, the cost that nobody modelled, includes the coaching infrastructure that nobody budgeted for.

Shamina Singh, president of the Mastercard Center for Inclusive Growth, described the scope of the shift: these systems bring "unprecedented levels of autonomy, complexity, and risk, requiring organisations to rethink traditional management strategies." Rethinking traditional management strategies includes rethinking the cost model that funds them. An enterprise that budgets coaching as a project cost will run out of budget before the agent runs out of drift.

> *"These systems bring unprecedented levels of autonomy, complexity, and risk, requiring organisations to rethink traditional management strategies."*
>
> **SHAMINA SINGH,**
> President, Mastercard Center for Inclusive Growth. MIT Sloan Management Review, "Agentic AI at Scale: Redefining Management for a Superhuman Workforce," 2025.

The practical implication is that every production AI agent needs a coaching allocation in the operating budget, not the project budget. Chapter 4 documented per-agent operating costs of $3,200 to $13,000 per month before accounting for the human oversight layer. An enterprise running twenty production agents without coaching allocations is not saving money. It is accumulating drift across twenty systems simultaneously, each compounding independently, with no funded mechanism to detect or respond. The CFO who understands this will fund the coaching infrastructure before it becomes a crisis. The CFO who does not will discover the gap when agents degrade and nobody has the mandate to fix them.

THE MANAGEMENT INFLECTION POINT

MIT Sloan Management Review and BCG stated the implication directly: "Agentic AI is not just a technology upgrade. It represents a management inflection point." The inflection is not in the technology layer. It is in how enterprises manage, govern, fund, and staff the systems that the technology produces. Agent coaching is where that inflection becomes operational.

> *"Agentic AI is not just a technology upgrade. It represents a management inflection point."*
>
> **MIT SLOAN MANAGEMENT REVIEW / BCG,**
> "The Emerging Agentic Enterprise: How Leaders Must Navigate a New Age of AI,"
> November 2025.

Coaching is not a standalone concept. It is how system stewardship, the discipline described in Chapter 5, manifests at the level of the individual agent. System stewardship governs the portfolio:

the aggregate health, economics, and governance posture across all AI systems in production. Agent coaching governs the agent: the specific, ongoing calibration of a single system's behaviour against the business outcome it was deployed to serve. The two operate at different altitudes but within the same discipline. A stewardship model without coaching has portfolio visibility but no mechanism for acting on what it sees at the agent level. A coaching practice without stewardship has agent-level intervention but no portfolio-level coordination.

The researchers found that the greatest gains come from "rethinking work from first principles, redesigning processes around hybrid teams of humans and AI agents." Coaching is the management practice for those hybrid teams. It is what the enterprise does when it accepts that agents are coworkers rather than tools and recognises that coworkers who make autonomous decisions in a changing environment need ongoing guidance, not a one-time briefing.

The counterargument is predictable: "We already monitor our agents." Most enterprises do. Monitoring tells you what happened. Coaching determines what to do about it. Monitoring is a sensor. Coaching is the response loop. The enterprise that has invested in observability tooling, logging dashboards, and alerting infrastructure has built the sensor array. What it has not built is the interpretive discipline that converts those signals into calibrated action. The gap is not instrumentation. It is interpretation and response.

Consider the typical enterprise response when an agent's performance degrades. The monitoring tool fires an alert. An engineer investigates. The engineer either retrains the model or adjusts a parameter, based on technical judgement alone. Nobody evaluates whether the degradation actually affected the business outcome. Nobody assesses whether the cost of intervention exceeds the cost of the drift. Nobody updates the governance posture to reflect what was learned. The intervention is reactive, technical, and disconnected from the business context. Coaching replaces that pattern with a continuous practice that is proactive, cross-functional, and outcome-aligned. The difference between the two is the difference between firefighting and fire prevention.

WHAT REMAINS

The discipline has been described. System stewardship replaces project management as the operating model for AI in production. The five control surfaces define what the steward must govern. The roles are emerging, visible in the 525 open positions that did not exist two years ago. And the core operational practice that distinguishes this discipline from everything that came before it, agent coaching, has been defined in this chapter.

Most enterprises have been budgeting training without budgeting coaching. The agents in production today were deployed with a training cost and no coaching allocation. The gap has been compounding since the first agent went live, quietly, in the space between the monitoring dashboard that shows the drift and the empty calendar where the coaching cadence should be.

The question that remains is whether the discipline works. The concepts are structurally sound. The evidence from MIT, BCG, Mastercard, and TÜV validates the need. The enterprises that are getting AI right are practising elements of this discipline, even if they do not call it by these names.

Agent coaching is not a training programme. It is the operating expense of keeping a probabilistic system aligned with the business outcome it was deployed to serve.

PART III:
Evidence

Better technology did not save them.
The operating discipline did.

VIJAYAN SEENISAMY

CHAPTER 9

What Good Looks Like

When researchers at MIT, Harvard Medical School, and eight other institutions deployed an agentic AI system for detecting adverse events in cancer immunotherapy patients, the system worked. It processed hundreds of clinical notes in minutes. It detected adverse events that manual review would have caught in days. The technology performed as designed.

The research team then published what they had learned, and the lesson had almost nothing to do with the technology.

Less than twenty percent of the effort had gone into the AI itself. Over eighty percent was consumed by data engineering, stakeholder alignment, governance design, workflow integration, and the continuous monitoring infrastructure required to keep the system reliable in a clinical environment where errors have consequences. The researchers did not describe this as an operational inconvenience. They described it as the work. The sociotechnical challenges, as they called them, were not obstacles on the path to deployment. They were the deployment.

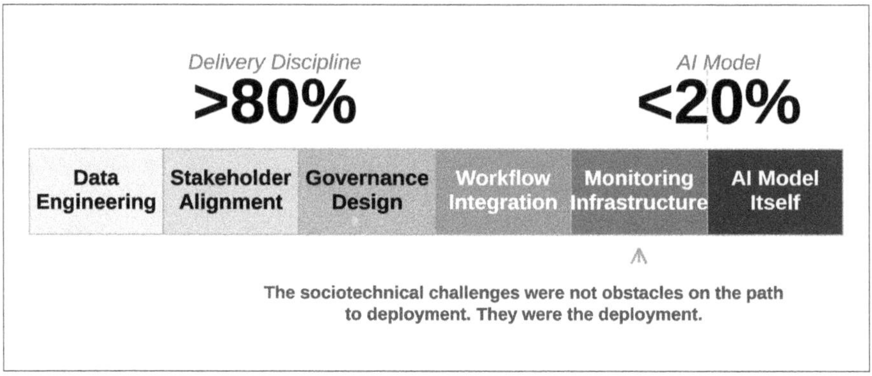

Less than twenty percent of the effort went into the AI itself. Over eighty percent was consumed by the delivery discipline that made the system reliable in production.

FIGURE 9.1
Where the Effort Actually Went

This book has spent eight chapters arguing that enterprise AI fails not because the technology is immature but because the delivery discipline does not exist. The MIT clinical team is evidence that the argument is correct. They succeeded because they built the discipline before they trusted the technology. They invested in governance at every step of the agentic process, continuous adaptive monitoring rather than static dashboards, structured data pipelines for agent compatibility, and named accountability at each stage. They practised system stewardship. They did not call it that.

The clinical system did not just work at launch. It continued to work, because the team built the infrastructure for it to continue working. The monitoring was not static. It tracked model drift, data drift, and surveillance system responsiveness simultaneously, using adaptive metrics rather than the fixed thresholds designed for deterministic systems. Governance was not a gate the system passed through once. It clarified risks at every step of the agentic process and remained active throughout operations. Every stage had a named accountable person, not because the methodology required it but because the team understood that a system making autonomous clinical decisions cannot operate without someone responsible for what it does after deployment.

None of the organisations in this chapter call what they built system stewardship. Each one arrived at elements of the discipline independently, because the discipline is not an invention. It is a recognition of what the enterprises getting AI right have already figured out, often painfully, often slowly, and always with more operational investment than any business case anticipated.

SEVEN YEARS OF DISCIPLINE

Starbucks began building Deep Brew in 2017. The AI platform launched in 2019. It is now in its seventh year of continuous AI production operations. In that time, Deep Brew has expanded from personalised recommendations to inventory management, staffing optimisation, store operations, and real estate selection. In 2024, Starbucks integrated generative AI into product development, using large language models to simulate flavour combinations and compress development cycles. In 2026, Green Dot Assist, an AI assistant for baristas built on Azure OpenAI, began rolling out across stores.

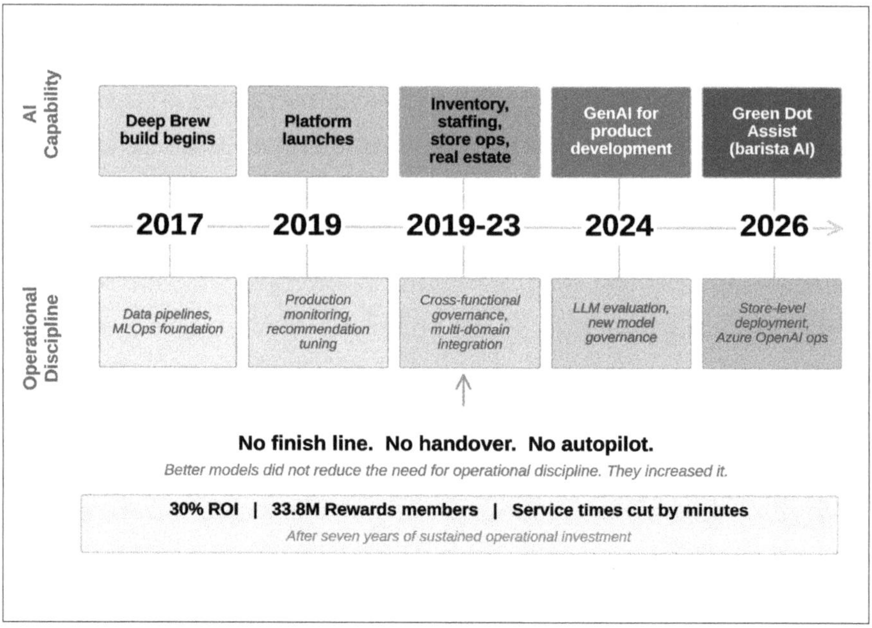

Both tracks deepen over seven years. Neither stops. The enterprises that treat AI as a project with a defined end state are not competing with Starbucks.

FIGURE 9.2
Seven Years of Discipline

The financial architecture is specific enough for the CFO to evaluate. Industry analysts estimate a 30 percent return on Starbucks' AI investment, with the Rewards program growing to 33.8 million active members by fiscal 2024. Industry analysts attribute meaningful incremental revenue to AI-driven personalisation, though Starbucks does not disclose the figure separately. The operational gains are more visible: AI-powered staffing and inventory optimisation contributed to measurable reductions in wait times during peak hours, and the broader effort has since cut average service times by minutes rather than seconds.

These numbers did not arrive in the first quarter. They did not arrive in the first year. They arrived after seven years of building the operational infrastructure that made the models productive at scale. That sequence matters more than any individual metric, because it reveals a pattern that contradicts the assumption most enterprise business cases are built on.

The assumption is that AI delivers value quickly after deployment. The Starbucks pattern shows the opposite. The returns were the compound result of seven years of sustained operational investment. And critically, as Starbucks expanded its AI capabilities across more business functions, the operational infrastructure grew with it. Better models and broader deployment did not reduce the need for MLOps, monitoring, and cross-functional governance. They increased it.

What is absent from the Starbucks story matters more than what is present. There is no moment where the AI programme was complete. There is no handover from a project team to an operations team that then ran the system on autopilot. There is no point where the investment in operational discipline decreased because the models had matured. The enterprises that treat AI as a project with a defined end state are not competing with Starbucks. They are competing with the version of themselves that will eventually discover why their AI investments have not produced equivalent returns.

A fair objection: Starbucks' returns were generated primarily by narrow AI systems, not the agentic systems this book focuses on. The objection is worth sitting with. Deep Brew's recommendation engine and inventory optimisation are closer to the deterministic end of the spectrum than the agentic frontier. But consider what the seven-year timeline reveals. If narrow AI, the simpler case, required seven years of sustained operational discipline to produce enterprise-scale returns, what does that imply for agentic systems that are more complex, more variable, and more autonomous? The operational investment required does not decrease as the technology becomes more probabilistic. It increases. Starbucks is not the evidence that the current model works. It is the evidence that even the simpler version of AI demanded a discipline most enterprises never built. The agentic frontier demands more.

THE ARCHITECTURAL CORRECTION

Not every enterprise gets the sequence right on the first attempt. Salesforce discovered this when early Agentforce deployments in heavily customised enterprise environments broke in ways the platform had not anticipated. Agents skipped steps. Business rules fired most of the time but not all. Edge cases that never surfaced in standard testing collided with legacy automation in ways that produced unpredictable behaviour. The pattern was precisely what Chapter 3 described: the Demo God Curse operating at platform scale. The technology worked in controlled conditions. Production conditions were not controlled.

What makes the Salesforce story instructive is not the failure. It is the response. Salesforce did not retreat from agentic AI. It shifted its entire deployment philosophy. The narrative moved from probabilistic execution back toward guardrails, deterministic automation layered underneath the agent, and a data-first design principle that amounted to an architectural correction, not a retreat. The lesson was specific: metadata first, models second. The enterprise environment must be legible to the agent before the agent can operate reliably within it. No amount of model capability compensates for an environment the model cannot read.

The correction maps directly to the integration architecture and governance surfaces described in Chapter 6. Salesforce discovered that agents deployed without structured integration into the existing automation landscape produced the exact failure modes this book has documented: drift, governance gaps, and unpredictable behaviour that no single monitoring tool could detect. The response was to build the missing discipline into the platform itself, requiring structured data, deterministic guardrails, and governance-by-design as prerequisites for agent deployment.

The Salesforce pattern provides something the Starbucks example does not: evidence that the discipline can be built after an initial failure, not only before one. Starbucks paid in patience. Salesforce paid in public correction. The enterprises that learn from both will pay less than either.

THE GOVERNANCE CORRELATION

The Starbucks evidence is longitudinal: one company, seven years, measurable returns. Deloitte's 2026 State of AI research, introduced in Chapter 3, provides the cross-sectional complement and a finding that should reframe how every enterprise executive thinks about AI governance.

Enterprises where senior leadership actively shapes AI governance achieve significantly greater business value than those delegating governance to technical teams alone. The correlation is not subtle. The organisations with the highest AI returns are not the ones with the best models or the largest data estates. They are the ones where governance is treated as a leadership discipline rather than a compliance obligation.

The Deloitte data adds a second dimension. Only one in five companies has a mature model for governance of autonomous AI agents. The number of companies with forty percent or more of AI projects in production is expected to double within the year. Investment is accelerating into a governance vacuum. The enterprises that have filled that vacuum are outperforming. The ones that have not are producing the failure rates documented in the first four chapters of this book.

Enterprise Technology Research confirmed the pattern from a different angle in early 2026. Their panel of enterprise IT leaders revealed a shift in how the most disciplined organisations are governing AI, captured precisely by one enterprise leader's description of the transformation: "Once we put all those data points on it, I think the governance became much more fact-based than emotion based. Initially people would take the smallest problem possible and just do it and voila, just to say, yeah, it works great. Now we're saying zoom out, define this thing, go in front of the execs, show them the big picture, and tell them what you're going to do."

> *"Once we put all those data points on it, the governance became much more fact-based than emotion based."*
>
> **ENTERPRISE IT LEADER,**
> ETR Tech Trends Feedback Panel, 2026.

That single quote captures the transition from what this book has called governance theatre to actual governance. The enterprises that are getting results are not the ones with the most impressive governance documentation. They are the ones that have moved from approving the smallest possible project to prove AI works to demanding upfront financial validation, defined ROI timelines, and measurable outcomes before a project is approved.

THE PATTERN

Four evidence sources, each with different methodologies, populations, and timeframes, arrived at the same structural finding. The enterprises producing measurable returns from AI share four characteristics that map directly to the discipline this book has described.

First, they invest more in the operating model than in the model itself. The MIT 80/20 split is the most dramatic expression, but the same ratio appears in every success pattern.

Second, they treat governance as an ongoing operational practice rather than a one-time compliance exercise. Deloitte's governance-led outperformance and ETR's shift to fact-based governance describe the same behaviour from different angles.

Third, they do not treat deployment as the finish line. Starbucks' seven-year timeline is the clearest demonstration. The MIT clinical team built continuous monitoring into their deployment from the beginning. The handover gap that produces failures in most enterprises did not exist.

Fourth, the financial returns followed the operational investment, not the technology investment. The discipline preceded the returns by years.

Measured against the five failure modes from Chapter 3, a structural inverse emerges. The Demo God Curse operates because pilot conditions are artificially controlled: curated data, low volume, the build team in the room monitoring every interaction. Every enterprise in this chapter built the opposite conditions from the start. The MIT team designed production-grade monitoring before deployment, not after the first incident. Starbucks scaled its operational infrastructure alongside its models for seven years. The governance-led enterprises in Deloitte's study treated oversight as continuous, not episodic. Where the Curse feeds on the gap between pilot and production, these enterprises closed that gap before the technology went live. The success pattern is not the absence of the Curse. It is its deliberate prevention.

THE SURVIVORSHIP OBJECTION

The counterargument is legitimate and worth addressing directly. These are success stories. Showing that successful enterprises practised discipline does not prove that discipline caused the success. Starbucks had the resources to invest in seven years of AI operations. MIT had ten institutions collaborating on a single deployment. Perhaps the discipline is a luxury of well-resourced organisations, not a causal factor.

The Deloitte data answers this objection. The governance-led outperformance finding is cross-sectional, not confined to a single well-resourced enterprise. The correlation between leadership-driven governance and business value holds across the full population, including organisations with modest AI budgets. Governance is not expensive. Absence of governance is expensive.

The ETR evidence reinforces the point from a different direction. The enterprises shifting to fact-based governance are not uniformly large or well-funded. They are the ones that learned from early failures that emotion-based governance, approving the smallest possible project to prove AI works, produces demos, not production systems. The shift to discipline is driven by pain, not resources.

There is a deeper structural answer as well. The diagnosis in the first four chapters of this book is not based on the presence of discipline in successful enterprises. It is based on the absence of discipline in failing ones. Ninety-five percent of enterprise AI pilots fail to reach reliable production. The cause is a delivery system designed for deterministic technology applied to probabilistic systems. When enterprises build the delivery discipline the technology requires, the technology delivers. When they do not, it does not.

WHAT THE EVIDENCE REQUIRES

What the evidence asks is simpler and harder. Whether the enterprise has built the operating model that makes AI productive, or whether it is still waiting for the technology to deliver value on its own.

An enterprise that has deployed AI agents without continuous evaluation, without economic governance at the task level, without defined accountability that survives project closure, and without the coordination discipline that connects all five control surfaces is not competing with the enterprises that have built this discipline. It is competing with the version of itself that will eventually build it, and every quarter of delay compounds the gap.

The financial implication is specific. The cost of operational discipline is visible and budgetable. The cost of its absence is invisible until it surfaces as a regulatory incident, a customer trust failure, or a budget variance that nobody can explain. The evidence in this chapter suggests that the return on delivery discipline is not marginal. It is the difference between AI programmes that produce enterprise outcomes and AI programmes that produce demos.

The question that follows is not whether to build the discipline. The evidence answers that. The question is whether there is time. Two major regulatory enforcement dates are weeks away.

The discipline preceded the returns. Not by weeks. By years. Every enterprise waiting for AI to deliver value before investing in operational discipline has the sequence backwards.

DISCIPLINE ELEMENT	MIT / HARVARD CLINICAL	STARBUCKS DEEP BREW	DELOITTE GOVERNANCE-LED	ETR FACT-BASED GOVERNANCE
Continuous evaluation	✓	✓	✓	✓
Economic governance	—	✓	—	✓
Accountability beyond project	✓	✓	—	—
Leadership-driven governance	✓	✓	✓	✓
Business outcome alignment	✓	✓	✓	✓
Cross-functional coordination	✓	✓	—	—
Discipline duration > 1 year	—	✓ (7 years)	—	—

✓ = evidenced in the pattern. — = not evidenced or not measured. No enterprise practises all elements. All practise multiple. The discipline is convergent even when the organisations are independent.

FIGURE 9.3
Four Success Patterns and the Discipline Elements They Practise

The regulatory clock
does not wait for your
operating model to catch up.
It is already running.

VIJAYAN SEENISAMY

CHAPTER 10

The Accountability Convergence

Gartner projects that fragmented AI regulation will quadruple by 2030, extending to seventy-five percent of the world's economies and driving over one billion dollars in total compliance spend (Gartner, 2025 AI prediction series). Separately, Gartner predicts that "death by AI" legal claims will exceed one thousand by the end of 2026, driven by deployments that lacked sufficient risk guardrails. These are not two data points about the same problem. They are two data points about two different accountability mechanisms arriving simultaneously.

That is the pattern enterprises are discovering. The general counsel asks for evidence that the company's AI systems comply with incoming automated decision-making provisions. The cyber insurer requests documentation of adversarial red-teaming and model-level risk assessments as a condition of renewal. The internal audit function flags AI governance as a material gap in its annual risk assessment. The board risk committee asks a question nobody can answer: who is accountable for the outputs of the AI agents currently in production? Four requests from four different functions, each asking the same question underneath: can this enterprise demonstrate continuous operational oversight of its AI systems?

Most cannot. Not because they are negligent, but because they have never built the infrastructure to produce the evidence. The AI systems are running. Some are performing well. None have the monitoring, governance, or accountability architecture that any of the four parties require.

This is not a regulatory problem. It is a convergence. Five independent forces, each operating on its own timeline and for its own reasons, are simultaneously demanding evidence of the same operational discipline. Regulators are one force. They are not the only one, and in many cases they are not the first to arrive. Insurers, auditors, boards, and the competitive market itself are all converging on the same set of requirements. The enterprise that builds the discipline produces the evidence once and satisfies all five. The enterprise that treats each demand as a separate compliance exercise will build five incomplete responses to a single structural gap.

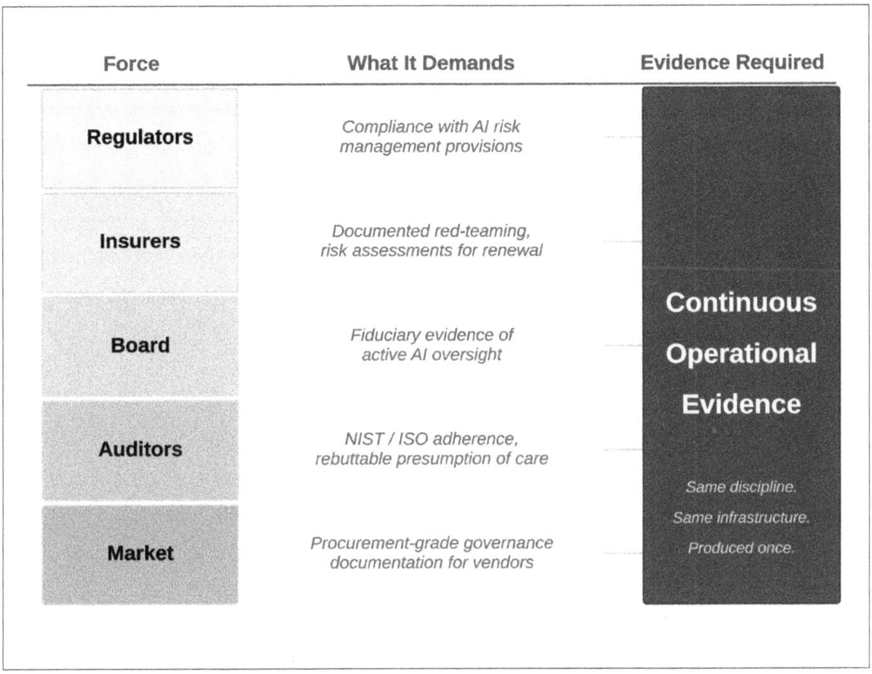

Five independent accountability forces, each operating on its own timeline and for its own reasons, converge on a single operational requirement. The enterprise that builds the discipline produces the evidence once and satisfies all five.

FIGURE 10.1
The Accountability Convergence

THE REGULATORY PRESSURE

The regulatory picture in 2026 is neither settled nor simple. It is moving fast enough that any CxO waiting for clarity before acting will find that enforcement arrived while they were waiting for the final rule.

Colorado's AI Act takes effect June 30, 2026. It applies to high-risk AI systems making or substantially influencing consequential decisions in employment, financial services, healthcare, housing, education, insurance, and legal services. Deployers must implement a risk management programme, complete impact assessments, conduct annual reviews, notify consumers when AI makes consequential decisions, and report algorithmic discrimination to the Attorney General within ninety days. Penalties reach twenty thousand dollars per violation, per consumer, per transaction.

The Act survived every attempt to weaken it. The American Bar Association noted in late 2025 that nothing fundamental changed despite lobbying by more than one hundred and fifty industry representatives. A federal executive order in December 2025 proposed preempting state AI laws inconsistent with federal policy, naming Colorado specifically. State laws remain enforceable until legal challenges are resolved. The practical guidance is to treat the Act as enforceable, because the compliance infrastructure required is identical to what enterprises need regardless of legislative outcome.

The EU AI Act operates on a different scale. Its August 2026 enforcement date activates provisions for high-risk AI systems, transparency obligations for general-purpose AI, and requirements that touch every enterprise using AI in customer-facing or employee-facing applications. Penalties reach thirty-five million euros or seven percent of worldwide revenue.

Beyond these two landmarks, the landscape is fragmenting. Texas signed the Responsible AI Governance Act in June 2025. Illinois amended its Human Rights Act to make discriminatory AI employment decisions a civil rights violation. The US Department of Justice announced an AI Litigation Task Force in January 2026. Australia's Privacy Act reforms, including automated decision-making provisions, take effect in December 2026. These are not future possibilities. They are current enforcement mechanisms.

JURISDICTION	ENFORCEMENT DATE	SCOPE	MAXIMUM PENALTY
Colorado (SB 24-205)	June 30, 2026	High-risk AI in consequential decisions	$20,000 per violation, per consumer, per transaction
EU AI Act (High-Risk)	August 2, 2026	High-risk AI systems, general-purpose AI transparency	€35M or 7% of worldwide revenue
Texas (HB 149)	Effective (signed June 2025)	AI for restricted purposes	$10,000–$200,000
Illinois (HB 3773)	Effective (signed August 2024)	Discriminatory AI in employment	Civil rights violation, existing IHRA procedures
US DOJ AI Litigation Task Force	Announced January 2026	Challenging state AI laws inconsistent with federal policy	Federal litigation, injunctive relief
Australia (Privacy Act Reforms)	December 2026	Automated decision-making transparency obligations	Existing laws apply (Privacy Act, Consumer Law)

Enforcement dates are current as of early 2026. Legislative amendments may alter timelines. The compliance infrastructure required is identical regardless of legislative outcome.

FIGURE 10.2
Regulatory Enforcement Timeline

THE INSURANCE ACCELERATION

The insurance market is not waiting for regulators. It is outpacing them.

Wilson Sonsini, the leading US technology-sector law firm, noted in early 2026 that insurers are requiring AI Security Riders with documented red-teaming and risk assessments as prerequisites for underwriting. This is not a future trend. It is a current condition of renewal for enterprises with AI systems in production. The cyber insurer is asking the same questions the regulator will ask, but the insurer is asking them now, and the consequence of a poor answer is not a fine. It is the loss of coverage at a moment when AI-related liability exposure is expanding.

The insurance market operates on a different logic than legislation. It does not need a political process, a lobbying cycle, or a comment period. It needs an actuarial basis for pricing risk. The insurer who cannot price AI operational risk accurately will either refuse to underwrite it or attach conditions that require the enterprise to demonstrate the operational discipline that makes the risk assessable. Both outcomes produce the same demand: show me the evidence that you are monitoring, governing, and maintaining accountability for your AI systems.

This is the most immediately consequential of the five forces. Regulatory enforcement is scheduled. Insurance renewal is annual. An enterprise that cannot demonstrate operational oversight of its AI portfolio may discover that the cost of insurance exceeds the cost of the discipline that would have reduced the premium.

THE BOARD'S FIDUCIARY QUESTION

Board-level AI governance is no longer a technology committee concern. It is a fiduciary obligation.

The pattern is identical to what happened with cybersecurity, compressed into a fraction of the time. The SEC first issued cybersecurity disclosure guidance in 2011. It took until 2018 for updated guidance. wMandatory board-level cybersecurity disclosure rules arrived in July 2023, with compliance required by December 2023 for large companies and June 2024 for smaller reporting companies. Twelve years from first guidance to enforceable board accountability. AI governance is travelling the same path in under five. The SEC's cybersecurity rules now require boards to demonstrate active oversight rather than passive awareness. The same expectation is already forming around AI, before the formal rules have arrived.

The question the board is asking is not technical. It is operational: does this enterprise have the governance infrastructure to ensure that its AI systems are behaving as intended, producing outcomes aligned with stated objectives, and operating within acceptable risk parameters? The board does not need to understand how the model works. The board needs to know that someone does, that the evidence is being generated continuously, and that accountability is named rather than assumed.

An enterprise practising system stewardship answers this question as a matter of routine. The five control surfaces produce the oversight evidence the board requires. The role architecture provides the named accountability. The coaching cadence demonstrates that the enterprise is actively managing its AI systems, not simply deploying them and hoping. For the board, the difference between an enterprise with this discipline and one without it is the difference between governance and hope. Fiduciary duty does not accommodate hope.

THE AUDIT BASELINE

Colorado's AI Act includes a provision that matters more to the practical reader than the penalty structure. Compliance with the NIST AI Risk Management Framework or ISO 42001 creates a rebuttable presumption of reasonable care. The enterprise demonstrating adherence to these standards has a legal defence: not immunity, but a structural argument that it exercised the duty of care the law requires.

The practical implication is that NIST and ISO are becoming the baseline expectation regardless of jurisdiction. An enterprise that adopts these frameworks is simultaneously building its regulatory defence for Colorado, strengthening its EU AI Act compliance posture, demonstrating the governance maturity that cyber insurers require, and producing the evidence trail that satisfies the board's fiduciary oversight. Multiple published governance frameworks exist globally, from Singapore's Model Governance Framework to the OWASP Agentic AI Top 10. They all converge on the same operational requirements.

These frameworks define what to govern. None of them define how to operationalise governance continuously in production. They are compliance-oriented: risk classification, audit logs, documentation, reporting. System stewardship is operations-oriented:

continuous evaluation, economic tracking, drift monitoring, agent health assessment, coached performance calibration. The governance frameworks tell the enterprise what evidence to produce. System stewardship is the operational discipline that produces it.

THE MARKET SIGNAL

The fifth force is the quietest and the most durable. The competitive market is developing its own accountability requirements, independent of regulation, and encoding them into procurement.

The evidence is already institutional. IEEE published Standard 3119-2025, a formal standard for the procurement of AI and automated decision systems, providing a step-by-step framework for identifying, assessing, and selecting AI vendors, including requirements for transparency documentation and ongoing monitoring. The EU published AI Model Contractual Clauses specifically for procurement of high-risk AI systems. The Australian government published AI Model Clauses in March 2025, covering both services where the vendor uses AI in delivery and procurement of AI systems themselves. The NIST AI Risk Management Framework's four pillars, Govern, Map, Measure, and Manage, now inform procurement expectations for vendors and partners in US federal agencies and regulated industries. States including Georgia have published procurement guidelines requiring vendors to demonstrate AI governance structures and conduct algorithmic impact assessments.

These are not aspirational frameworks. They are conditions of sale. The enterprise customer evaluating two vendors, one with documented AI governance and one without, is making the same risk calculation the insurer makes. The partner assessing whether to integrate with an enterprise's AI systems is asking the same accountability questions the board asks. When procurement departments embed AI governance requirements into RFPs and vendor assessments, the market is enforcing a standard that no legislature voted on and no regulator mandated. It is enforcing it through the oldest mechanism in commerce: the decision to buy or not to buy.

These questions do not arrive on a regulatory timeline. They arrive on a transaction timeline. Every interaction with a customer, partner, or counterparty is an implicit audit of whether the enterprise can account for what its AI systems are doing. The enterprises that built the discipline are producing the evidence as a byproduct of operations. Everyone else is discovering the gap one relationship at a time.

THE EVIDENCE THAT CANNOT BE MANUFACTURED

This is the structural argument beneath the convergence. All five forces, regulators, insurers, boards, auditors, and the market, demand the same kind of evidence: continuous, operational, timestamped, and attributable. And this evidence has a property that distinguishes it from every other compliance artefact the enterprise has ever produced. It accumulates. It cannot be manufactured retroactively.

Consider what a regulatory audit of an AI system in production actually requires. The auditor asks: what is this system doing? How do you know it is performing within acceptable parameters? When was it last evaluated? Who is accountable for its outputs? What happens when it drifts outside acceptable range? Can you produce the evidence trail showing continuous oversight?

An enterprise practising system stewardship can answer every one of those questions from existing operational data. The observability surface generates the performance evidence. The governance surface produces the compliance documentation. The orchestration surface demonstrates named accountability and defined review cadence. The business alignment surface shows ongoing value tracking. The evidence is a byproduct of the operating discipline, not a separate compliance exercise.

An enterprise that has not built this discipline cannot produce the evidence retroactively. Compliance documentation assembled after the fact, reconstructed from scattered logs and inferred governance trails, does not demonstrate continuous oversight. It demonstrates retrospective documentation. The auditor, the insurer, and the board know the difference. An enterprise that begins building continuous monitoring three months before an enforcement date will have three months of evidence. An enterprise that has been practising system stewardship for eighteen months will have eighteen months of evidence. The depth of the evidence trail is the discipline made visible.

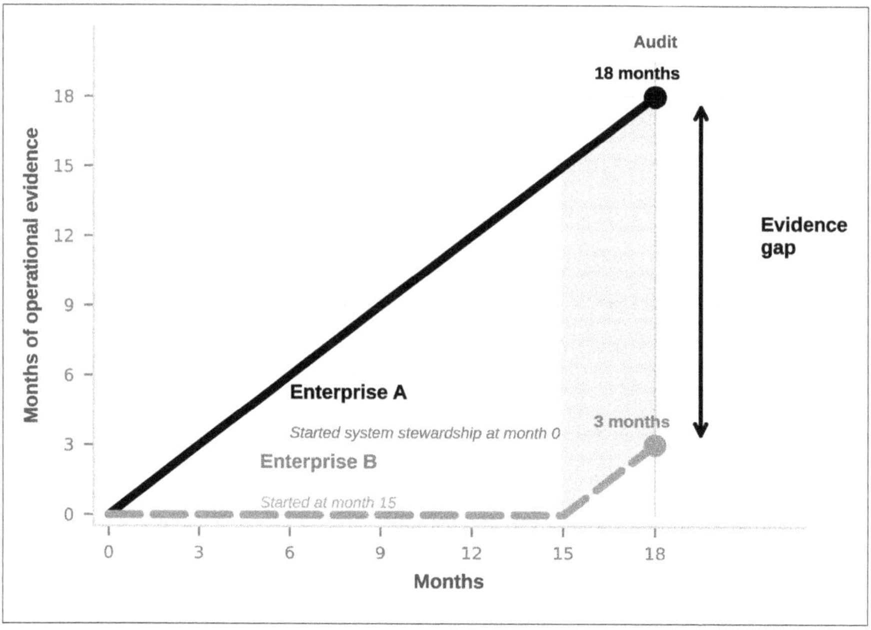

Enterprise A has practised system stewardship for eighteen months. Enterprise B started the same discipline three months before the audit. Both invested the same effort. Only time separates them.

FIGURE 10.3
The Evidence Accumulation Gap

> *The evidence accumulates as a byproduct of the discipline, not as a response to the deadline. An enterprise cannot manufacture eighteen months of continuous oversight in the weeks before the auditor arrives. The investment is not in compliance. It is in time.*

This convergence creates what Andy Grove, the former Intel CEO, called a strategic inflection point: a moment where the cost of action after the point is structurally higher than the cost of action before it. The accountability convergence is that point for enterprise AI. Before the convergence, building operational discipline is an investment in reliability. After it, the same investment becomes a remediation exercise, compressed into shorter timelines, under external pressure, with an evidence gap that cannot be closed by effort alone. The enterprise that recognises the inflection point before it can be proven has the advantage. The enterprise that waits for proof, for the audit finding, the insurance denial, the board question that nobody can answer, discovers that the window for building the evidence trail at a manageable pace has already closed. The structural property of evidence accumulation means that delay does not just defer cost. It eliminates options. Every quarter of inaction is a quarter of evidence that will never exist.

WHAT THIS MEANS FOR THE INVESTMENT

The discipline described in this book was not designed for compliance. It was designed for operational reliability. Compliance is a consequence, not the objective. An enterprise that monitors its AI systems continuously, tracks their economics, governs their behaviour, and coaches their performance is coincidentally producing every piece of evidence a regulator, auditor, insurer, or board will ask for. The discipline serves the business first. It serves the five accountability forces as a byproduct.

That distinction matters for how the CxO positions the investment internally. System stewardship is not a compliance cost. It is an operational capability that happens to produce compliance evidence. The CFO who funds it as a compliance line item will underfund it, because compliance budgets are defensive and minimal. The CFO who funds it as an operational capability will size it correctly, because operational budgets are scaled to the portfolio they govern. The accountability convergence creates urgency. The operating discipline creates value. Both lead to the same investment. The framing determines whether it is funded properly.

The counterargument is that the landscape is still moving and it would be prudent to wait for clarity before investing. Colorado may be amended. The EU may simplify. Insurers may soften their requirements. Boards may defer. The logic is familiar: why build for demands that might change?

The logic fails because the demands are converging, not diverging. Every regulatory framework, every insurance requirement, every audit standard, and every board governance expectation converges on the same operational capabilities: continuous monitoring, named accountability, audit trails, risk classification, impact assessments. Building for one prepares you for all. Building for none leaves you exposed to all. And the evidence that each of them will require cannot be compressed. It is measured in months of operational data, not in the quality of the documentation produced the week before the audit.

The readiness scorecard
does not tell you what to build.
It tells you what you
have been avoiding.

VIJAYAN SEENISAMY

CHAPTER 11

Where You Stand

What follows is a readiness assessment. Ten questions, two per control surface, designed to be answered in a leadership meeting without consultants, external assessors, or specialised tools. The questions are diagnostic, not exhaustive. They will not tell you everything. They will tell you enough to identify your deepest gaps and your most urgent priorities.

FOUR STAGES OF DELIVERY MATURITY

Before answering the ten questions, the enterprise needs the measurement framework. The AI Role Operating Framework™ defines four maturity stages that describe how an enterprise's AI delivery capability progresses. Every enterprise sits in one of these stages, and different control surfaces within the same enterprise often sit in different stages simultaneously.

STAGE	WHAT IT LOOKS LIKE IN PRACTICE
Ad-Hoc	No formal delivery discipline. Agents are deployed based on demos that worked. No named owners in production. No evaluation cadence. Incident response is reactive. Regulated use cases should not progress to production at this stage.
Repeatable	Templates and early risk checks are emerging. Some agents have named owners. Basic logging exists but evaluation is inconsistent. Governance is present but not embedded in operational rhythm. Scaling beyond pilots remains risky.
Scalable	Policies for evaluation, drift detection, and rollback are in place. An AI Delivery Manager or equivalent owns reliability. Formal orchestration connects technical and business teams. Shared dashboards exist. Expansion within a business unit becomes safe.
Enterprise Ready	AI delivery is embedded in enterprise governance. Board-level visibility into AI portfolio performance. Full observability across reliability, safety, economics, adoption, and drift. AI systems are treated as critical enterprise infrastructure, not experiments.

The Production-Ready Threshold is the entry point to Scalable. Enterprises below this threshold have identifiable gaps that create measurable risk in production AI operations.

FIGURE 11.1
Four Maturity Stages

Most enterprises that believe they are Scalable discover, when they answer the questions honestly, that they are in the upper range of Repeatable. The gap between having policies and having embedded operational discipline is wider than it appears on paper. The questions that follow are designed to surface that gap.

THE TEN QUESTIONS

Answer each question honestly based on what is true today. Not the planned state. Not the state described in the last board presentation. Not the state the team aspires to reach. The value of this assessment depends entirely on honesty about current capability.

For each question, score the enterprise using the readiness key below the assessment.

BUSINESS ALIGNMENT

QUESTION 1: Can you name the specific business lever that each production AI agent is measured against? Not the use case description from the original business case, but the live metric that someone reviews on a defined schedule to confirm the agent is still delivering value.

QUESTION 2: When was the last time someone formally reviewed whether each production agent is still delivering measurable value against its original business case?

INTEGRATION ARCHITECTURE

QUESTION 3: Do your production AI agents share common infrastructure for authentication, logging, and data access, or does each agent operate on its own technical stack?

QUESTION 4: If a production agent needed to be rolled back to a previous state or shut down entirely, could your team execute that within two hours?

GOVERNANCE AND COMPLIANCE

QUESTION 5: Is there a named individual, not a committee, not a team, not a department, accountable for each production AI agent's behaviour in production right now?

QUESTION 6: Does your governance framework evaluate agent behaviour continuously during production, or only at deployment and during scheduled reviews?

OBSERVABILITY AND EVALUATION

QUESTION 7: Can you produce, today, the task success rate for each production agent over the past thirty days? Not uptime. Not throughput. The percentage of tasks the agent completed correctly against a defined evaluation standard.

QUESTION 8: Do you know the cost per successful outcome for each production agent, not the monthly infrastructure bill, but the actual cost of each task the agent completes correctly?

ORCHESTRATION AND OPERATIONS

QUESTION 9: Is there a defined cadence, weekly, fortnightly, or otherwise, for reviewing agent performance across your portfolio, attended by the roles described in Chapter 7?

QUESTION 10: If a production agent generated a harmful, inaccurate, or non-compliant output at 2am on a Sunday, who would be notified and what documented process would they follow?

SCORING YOUR READINESS

For each question, choose the statement that most honestly describes the enterprise today.

SCORE	WHAT IT MEANS
Red	The enterprise cannot answer this question, or the answer reveals a capability that has not been built.
Amber	A partial answer exists, or the capability is present for some agents but not consistently across the portfolio.
Green	The answer is confident with specific evidence: named individuals, defined cadences, measurable data.

Record the score for each question. Then read the surface-level pattern: two reds in a pair means that control surface is not operational. Two greens means it is. Any other combination means the surface exists in fragments but is not reliable.

CONTROL SURFACE	Q	SCORE	Q	SCORE	SURFACE
Business Alignment	1		2		
Integration Architecture	3		4		
Governance and Compliance	5		6		
Observability and Evaluation	7		8		
Orchestration and Operations	9		10		

Fill in each cell. The rightmost column is the surface-level reading. Two greens = operational. Any red = gap. The surface with the most red touching the most production agents is the first priority.

FIGURE 11.2
Readiness Scorecard

WHAT THE QUESTIONS SURFACE

The ten questions are deliberately chosen. Each tests a specific failure point that this book has diagnosed.

Questions 1 and 2 test whether the enterprise has crossed from project launch to production governance. The gap between a use case description and a live performance metric is the gap between a project that launched and a system that is governed. If the answer to Question 1 is "we track usage" or "we know it is working because nobody has complained," the business alignment surface is not operational. That is the Demo God Curse from Chapter 3 in its most common production form: an agent operating on inherited confidence, not evidence.

Questions 3 and 4 test whether the enterprise built enough architecture to deploy, or enough to recover. When each agent has its own authentication, its own logging pipeline, and its own data access patterns, the enterprise can observe individual agents in isolation but cannot observe the portfolio. It cannot detect cross-agent risks, enforce consistent security policies, or produce the portfolio-level cost data that Chapter 4 described as essential. Rollback readiness is the stress test. In probabilistic systems, rollback depends on runtime context, not just code. An enterprise that cannot roll back an agent within two hours has built enough architecture to deploy but not enough to operate.

Questions 5 and 6 test whether accountability is structural or diffused. A committee cannot own an agent's behaviour. A shared Slack channel cannot own an agent's behaviour. Question 5 asks whether a single name is attached to each agent's production conduct. Question 6 tests the gap between operational governance and governance theatre: frameworks that evaluate the system at deployment, then do not evaluate again until the next scheduled review. The interval between reviews is the interval during which the system can drift without detection.

Questions 7 and 8 test the distinction between monitoring and evaluation. An agent can have one hundred percent uptime and fifty percent task accuracy. Without evaluation, the enterprise sees the uptime and misses the accuracy.

Question 8 tests visibility into the economics described in Chapter 4. Cost per successful outcome divides total operating cost by the number of tasks completed to the required standard. Without it, the enterprise cannot determine whether the agent has crossed into negative unit economics, the inversion point where the agent task costs more than the human work it replaced. The economics feel fine at pilot scale because volumes are low and cost is buried in a project budget. At production scale, the inversion surfaces in the CFO's quarterly variance analysis.

Questions 9 and 10 test the operating rhythm. The difference between Repeatable and Scalable is often a single structural element: a regular cadence where the AI Delivery Manager, AgentOps Lead, AI Architect, and AI Product Manager review portfolio performance together. Without that cadence, each role operates in isolation, making local decisions without portfolio-level visibility. Question 10 is the stress test for the entire model. Most enterprises discover their incident response process is improvised when they actually need it.

THE GOVERNANCE OBJECTION

The most common objection at this point is that the enterprise already has governance. The AI ethics board meets quarterly. The risk framework was updated last year. The compliance team reviewed the deployment. The objection is sincere, and it misses the point.

The ten questions do not test whether governance exists. They test whether governance operates continuously in production. An ethics board that meets quarterly has a ninety-day blind spot between meetings. A risk framework updated at deployment has not been tested against the system's current behaviour. A compliance review at launch does not produce evidence of ongoing oversight.

> *The distinction is not between governed and ungoverned. It is between governance that evaluates the system as it is now and governance that evaluated the system as it was then.*

Four out of five enterprises still lack a mature governance model for autonomous agents (Deloitte, State of AI in the Enterprise, 2026). Meanwhile, the number of companies pushing forty percent or more of AI projects into production is expected to double within the year. Investment is accelerating into a governance vacuum. Most enterprises, when they answer these ten questions honestly, discover they have the second kind of governance. The finding confirms the pattern is not exceptional. It is the norm.

THE TYPICAL PATTERN

The most common readiness profile is not uniformly weak. It is lopsided. Integration and observability tend to score higher, because engineering teams built them as part of the deployment process. Business alignment, governance, and orchestration tend to score lower, because nobody owns them after the project closes. The enterprise has strong technical foundations and weak operational discipline layered on top.

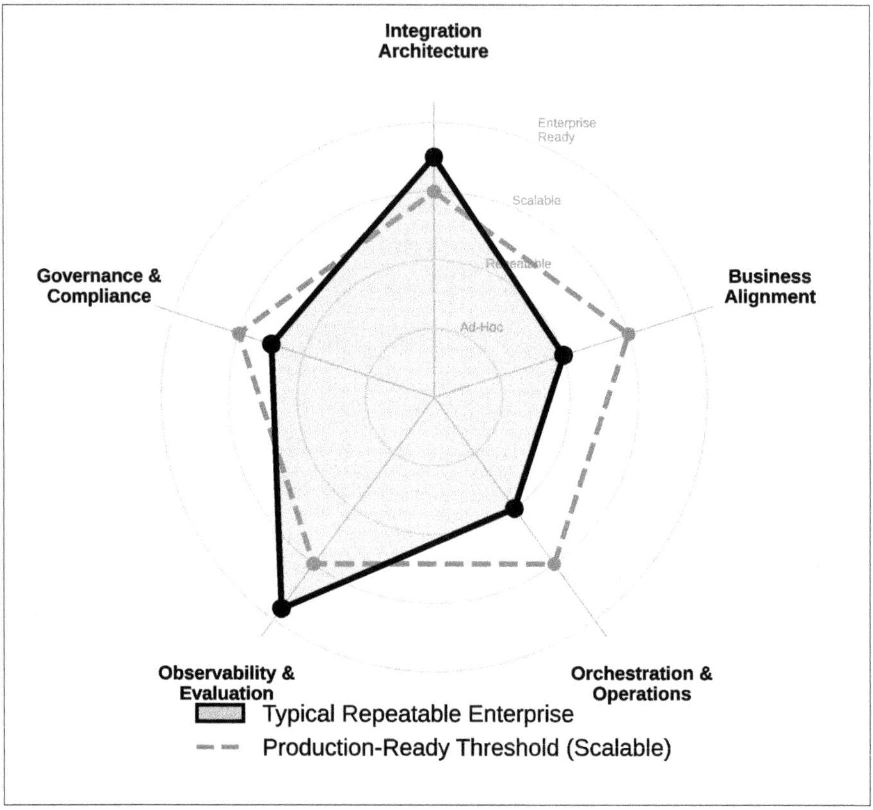

FIGURE 11.3
Typical Repeatable Enterprise vs. Production-Ready Target

The shape of the gap matters more than the depth of any single surface. An enterprise with uniformly amber scores has a different problem than an enterprise with three greens and two reds. The first needs operational maturity across the board. The second has specific structural gaps that create concentrated risk. The prioritisation rule is the same in both cases: the surface with the lowest maturity that touches the most production agents is the first priority. Start where the exposure is widest and the maturity is lowest.

That intersection is where the next production incident is most likely to originate.

> *The assessment does not tell you what to do. It tells you where you are. The value is in the honesty, not in the score.*

The discipline came first.
The scale came later.

VIJAYAN SEENISAMY

CHAPTER 12

The Five-Agent Test

Everything in this book converges on a practical question: what do you do on Monday morning?

Not next quarter. Not after the transformation programme is approved. Monday. The answer is smaller than you expect and more revealing than any enterprise-wide assessment. Pick five agents. The five that matter most to your enterprise. Spend one week asking the questions nobody has asked about them. Write down what you find.

WHICH FIVE

The selection is not a methodology. It is a judgment call the CIO or CAIO can make in a single conversation. Choose the five production AI agents that touch the most revenue, the most customers, or the most regulated processes. If the list is not obvious, apply a simpler filter: pick the five where a silent failure would eventually reach the board. Every enterprise has five. Most have more. Five is enough to reveal a pattern.

THE FIVE CONVERSATIONS

Each conversation maps to one of the five control surfaces described in Chapter 6. Each will surface a specific finding. The findings are predictable, because the structural gaps that produced them are the same gaps this book has diagnosed across eleven chapters. What follows is not a script. It is what the questions will surface.

THE BUSINESS OWNER

Find the person accountable for the business process each agent touches. Ask one question: what metric confirms that this agent is still delivering value against its original business case?

In most enterprises, the answer is one of three things. The business owner names a usage metric, not an outcome metric. "We know people are using it" is not evidence of value. Or the business owner references the pilot results, which were produced under conditions that no longer exist. Or the business owner does not know, because the business case was written by the project team, and the project team moved on nine months ago.

That is the Demo God Curse from Chapter 3 in its production form. The agent is operating on inherited confidence from a pilot that proved it could work, not evidence that it is working. The gap between those two statements is the gap the business alignment surface was designed to close.

THE INFRASTRUCTURE LEAD

Find the person who manages the technical environment these agents operate in. Ask: if we needed to roll back any of these agents to a previous state or shut one down entirely, could your team execute that within two hours?

The typical answer: for one or two agents, probably. For the others, it depends. Each agent was built by a different team, on a different stack, with different authentication and logging patterns. Rollback was never designed because the deployment was treated as a one-way event. The enterprise built enough architecture to deploy. It did not build enough to recover.

When each agent operates on its own technical stack, the enterprise can observe individual agents in isolation but cannot observe the portfolio. It cannot detect cross-agent risks, enforce consistent security policies, or produce the portfolio-level cost data that Chapter 4 described as essential.

THE PERSON ACCOUNTABLE

For each of the five agents, ask: who, by name, is accountable for this agent's behaviour in production right now? Not which team. Not which department. A name.

This is the conversation where the gaps become personal. The project team's mandate ended at deployment. The operations team was never formally briefed. The business owner assumed the technology team was monitoring it. The technology team assumed the business was reviewing outcomes. The agent has been running in production for months without a single person whose job description includes ensuring it behaves correctly.

The role exists in negative space. Formalising it does not add overhead. It makes visible the accountability that should have existed from the day the agent went live. Chapter 7 described this as the AI Delivery Manager's core function. In most enterprises, nobody occupies that function. The five-agent test makes the absence undeniable.

THE EVALUATOR

Ask: can anyone produce the task success rate for each of these five agents over the past thirty days? Not uptime. Not throughput. The percentage of tasks each agent completed correctly against a defined evaluation standard.

The most common discovery: the evaluation standard does not exist. The agent was deployed with acceptance criteria for the pilot phase. Nobody translated those criteria into production evaluation metrics. The monitoring infrastructure tracks whether the agent is running. It does not track whether the agent is right. An agent can have one hundred percent uptime and fifty percent task accuracy. Without evaluation, the enterprise sees the uptime and misses the accuracy.

Then ask: what does each agent cost per successful outcome? Not the monthly infrastructure bill. The actual cost of each task the agent completes correctly. This is the question from Chapter 4 that surfaces negative unit economics, the inversion point where the agent costs more per task than the human process it replaced. In most enterprises, nobody has calculated this number because the financial governance model was not designed to track cost at the task level. That question is also the one to take to your CFO. Chapter 4 documented TCO underestimation of forty to sixty percent. The inability to answer it creates the same mandate through a different door.

THE INCIDENT RESPONDER

Ask: if one of these agents generated a harmful, inaccurate, or noncompliant output at 2am on a Sunday, who would be notified and what documented process would they follow?

Most enterprises discover their incident response process is improvised when they actually test the question. The person who would be called is not formally assigned. The process that would be followed does not exist in writing. The escalation path depends on who happens to notice first. This is not negligence. It is the structural consequence of deploying production systems through a project model that ended at go-live.

SURFACE	WHO TO TALK TO	WHAT YOU WILL FIND
Business Alignment	Business process owner	Pilot metrics not translated to production. No one is reviewing whether the agent still delivers value against its original business case.
Integration Architecture	Infrastructure lead	Rollback not designed. Each agent built on its own stack. Portfolio-level visibility does not exist.
Governance & Compliance	The person "accountable"	No named individual. Accountability dissolved when the project team moved on. The agent runs without an owner.
Observability & Evaluation	Technical lead / data team	Task success rate unknown. Cost per successful outcome never calculated. Uptime is monitored. Output quality is not.
Orchestration & Operations	Whoever gets called when it breaks	Process is improvised. No documented incident response. Escalation depends on who notices first.

Five conversations. Five surfaces. One week. The findings will be uncomfortable. They will also be invisible until someone looks.

FIGURE 12.1
The Five Conversations

THE SCORECARD

The output from these conversations is a single page. Five agents across. Five surfaces down. Each cell scored red, amber, or green based on what you heard.

CONTROL SURFACE	AGENT 1	AGENT 2	AGENT 3	AGENT 4	AGENT 5
Business Alignment					
Integration Architecture					
Governance & Compliance					
Observability & Evaluation					
Orchestration & Operations					

Score each cell red, amber, or green. The surfaces that are consistently red across all five agents are not five individual gaps. They are one structural gap repeated five times.

FIGURE 12.2
The Five-Agent Scorecard

The pattern will be visible in thirty seconds. That pattern is the enterprise's delivery failure mode. It exists because the same project-based deployment model produced all five agents. The agents are different. The gap that produced them is identical.

That scorecard is what goes to the CIO. Not as a recommendation. As a finding. The CIO looks at consistent red cells across accountability, evaluation, and economics, and the conversation changes from "should we invest in AI governance" to "how did we let this happen."

FIGURE 12.3
The Five-Agent Test Timeline

WHAT YOU WILL NOT FIND

You will not find negligence. You will find the structural consequence of deploying probabilistic systems through a delivery model that was designed to end at go-live. The people who built these agents did their jobs. The people who operate the business processes these agents touch are doing their jobs. The gap is not between people. It is between the operating model the enterprise has and the operating model the technology requires. That gap has a name. This book gave it one in Chapter 2. The five-agent test is where the category error stops being a diagnosis and becomes visible in your own enterprise.

THE WAY OUT

This book opened with a trap. Ninety-five percent of enterprise AI deployments fail to reach reliable production. The cause is not the technology. It is the absence of a delivery discipline designed for technology that behaves probabilistically, learns continuously, and operates autonomously.

Eleven chapters later, the discipline exists. Five control surfaces. A role architecture. A coaching practice. A regulatory map. A readiness assessment. The diagnosis is complete.

The discipline does not start with a transformation programme. It starts with five conversations that make the invisible visible. Starbucks did not begin with a seven-year plan for Deep Brew. It began with one use case in 2017. The discipline came first. The scale came later. The five-agent test follows the same logic. The enterprise that runs it this week will know, by Friday, what it did not know on Monday. That knowledge is the foundation. Everything else, the roles, the cadences, the governance, the full assessment, builds on top of a single decision: the decision to look.

The trap is not that enterprises lack the technology. It is that they have never looked at what happens after deployment. The five-agent test is the decision to look. Everything changes after that.

NOTES

The data points, research findings, and attributed claims throughout this book are sourced from publicly available research and industry reports. All sources are cited inline where they appear. This section provides the full reference for each source, grouped by chapter.

CHAPTER 1: THE PILOT TRAP

- **MIT Sloan Management Review / S&P Global.** NANDA Initiative, 2025. 150 executive interviews, 350-employee survey, 300 public AI deployments.

- **S&P Global Market Intelligence.** Enterprise AI Abandonment Tracking, 2025.

- **Camunda / Coleman Parkes.** 2026 State of Agentic Orchestration and Automation. 1,150 senior IT decision makers, January 2026.

- **Gartner.** Worldwide AI Spending Forecast, January 2026. $2.52 trillion projected for 2026, 44% increase year-over-year.

- **ADAPT.** CFO Edge Research, November 2025. Australian CFO survey: 77% report not effectively realising AI value; 4% describe their organisation as "very effective" at AI value delivery.

- **MIT Sloan Management Review / BCG.** "The Emerging Agentic Enterprise: How Leaders Must Navigate a New Age of AI," November 2025. 2,102 respondents.

CHAPTER 2: THE CATEGORY ERROR

- **MIT Sloan Management Review / BCG.** "The Emerging Agentic Enterprise: How Leaders Must Navigate a New Age of AI," November 2025. 2,102 respondents.

- **McKinsey.** "The State of AI 2025." 1,993 participants, 105 nations, November 2025.

- **Camunda.** 2026 State of Agentic Orchestration and Automation, January 2026. 1,150 leaders.

- **Kate Kellogg, MIT Sloan.** "5 Heavy Lifts for Agentic AI," February 2026. Research on sociotechnical challenges of agentic AI deployment, including the requirement for adaptive monitoring and continuous evaluation.

- **MIT / Harvard Medical School / eight additional institutions.** Agentic AI deployment for cancer immunotherapy adverse event surveillance, 2026. Less than 20% of effort on AI model; over 80% on data engineering, governance, integration, monitoring, and organisational change.

CHAPTER 3: FIVE WAYS ENTERPRISE AI FAILS

- **Air Canada.** Chatbot liability ruling, 2024. Airline held legally liable for incorrect information provided by its AI chatbot to a customer.

- **Klarna.** AI customer service replacement and subsequent rehiring after customer satisfaction declined.

- **McDonald's.** AI hiring chatbot data exposure incident, 64 million job applications vulnerable.

- **LangChain.** State of Agent Engineering, December 2025. 1,300+ AI practitioners surveyed. Finding: 89% of organisations had implemented some form of observability for their agents, but only 52% had addressed evaluation beyond basic monitoring.

- **IBM.** 2025 Data Breach Report. Ponemon Institute, 600 organisations researched. Finding: 13% of organisations reported breaches of AI models or applications; of those, 97% lacked proper AI access controls. Across all breached organisations, 63% lacked AI governance policies entirely.

- **Deloitte.** State of AI in the Enterprise, 2026. 3,235 leaders across 24 countries. Finding: only one in five enterprises has a mature governance model for autonomous AI agents; enterprises with leadership-driven governance achieve significantly greater business value.

- **ADAPT.** CFO Edge Research, November 2025. Australian data on AI investment and value realisation gaps.

- **McKinsey.** "The State of AI 2025." 1,993 participants, 105 nations, November 2025. Finding: fewer than 40% of organisations report any formal governance for AI deployment.

- **CB Insights.** Executive survey, 2025. 59 executives surveyed. Finding: 40% could not track, or were unaware of, the actual return on investment for their AI agents.

- **Kate Kellogg, MIT Sloan.** Research confirming that static monitoring designed for deterministic systems cannot detect drift in probabilistic AI outputs.

- **BCG.** Research on enterprise AI deployment: 10% of the challenge is the technology, 20% is the data, 70% is people and processes.

- **Starbucks / Deep Brew.** Seven years of continuous AI production operations across personalisation, inventory, staffing, and store operations. Referenced as evidence that operational discipline grows with capability.

CHAPTER 4: THE ECONOMICS NOBODY MODELLED

- **AnalyticsWeek.** January 2026 report on enterprise AI inference cost escalation: inference bills arriving at five times original cloud budget allocations.

- **CB Insights.** AI Agent ROI Executive Survey, Q4 2025. Finding: 40% of enterprises cannot track ROI on their AI agents.

- **Starbucks / Deep Brew.** Industry analysts estimate a 30% return on AI investment, with Rewards programme growing to 33.8 million active members by fiscal Q4 2024. Starbucks Q4 and Full Fiscal Year 2024 Results, Nasdaq, October 30, 2024.

CHAPTER 5: FROM PROJECT MANAGEMENT TO SYSTEM STEWARDSHIP

- **MIT / Harvard Medical School / eight additional institutions.** Agentic AI deployment for cancer immunotherapy adverse event surveillance, 2026. Referenced for 80/20 effort split.

- **BCG.** "How Agents Are Accelerating the Next Wave of AI Value Creation," December 2025.

- **ETR (Enterprise Technology Research).** AI Product Series, February 2026. Panel of enterprise IT leaders on the shift from experimentation to disciplined execution.

- **OpenAI.** Frontier Alliances with McKinsey, BCG, Accenture, Capgemini, February 2026. Multi-year partnerships to build enterprise AI delivery capability.

- **Deloitte.** State of AI in the Enterprise, 2026. Referenced for governance-led outperformance finding.

- **Gartner.** Hype Cycle and Magic Quadrant methodology. Referenced as industry analysis that describes markets but does not codify operational disciplines.

CHAPTER 6: THE FIVE CONTROL SURFACES

- **CB Insights.** AI Agent ROI Executive Survey, Q4 2025. Finding: 40% of enterprises cannot track ROI on AI agents.

- **Starbucks.** 'DeepBrew 2.0: Starbucks ML Platform.' Databricks Data + AI Summit, 2024.

- **ADAPT.** CIO Edge Research, 2025. Finding: only 47% of key business processes operate in real time; only 50% of employees have access to the data they need.

- **IBM.** Cost of a Data Breach Report, 2025. Same source as Chapter 3. Referenced for AI access control and governance policy findings.

CHAPTER 7: THE ROLES THAT DO NOT EXIST YET

- **LinkedIn.** Job market data, early 2025. 525+ open positions with "AI Delivery Manager" in the title globally. Salary range from approximately $48,000 to $412,000, an eightfold spread.

- **Shamina Singh, President, Mastercard Center for Inclusive Growth.** Quoted in MIT Sloan Management Review, "Agentic AI at Scale: Redefining Management for a Superhuman Workforce," 2025. Referenced for "unprecedented levels of autonomy, complexity, and risk."

CHAPTER 8: AGENT COACHING, NOT AGENT TRAINING

- **Vibhor Rastogi, Head of AI and APAC Investments, Citi Ventures.** Quoted in MIT Sloan Management Review / BCG, "The Emerging Agentic Enterprise: How Leaders Must Navigate a New Age of AI," November 2025. Referenced for "treated like coworkers who need to be trained, coached, supervised."

- **Franziska Weindauer, TUV AI.Lab.** Quoted in MIT Sloan Management Review, "Agentic AI at Scale: Redefining Management for a Superhuman Workforce," 2025. Referenced for "these systems make decisions on their own, and those decisions can directly impact people, workflows, and critical decisions."

- **MIT Sloan Management Review / BCG.** "The Emerging Agentic Enterprise," November 2025. Referenced for "excessive supervision negates autonomy benefits; insufficient oversight creates operational, compliance, and reputational risks."

- **Shamina Singh, President, Mastercard Center for Inclusive Growth.** Quoted in MIT Sloan Management Review, 2025. Referenced for "unprecedented levels of autonomy, complexity, and risk, requiring organisations to rethink traditional management strategies."

- **MIT Sloan Management Review / BCG.** "The Emerging Agentic Enterprise," November 2025. Referenced for "agentic AI is not just a technology upgrade. It represents a management inflection point."

- **BCG.** Research on enterprise AI deployment. Referenced for the tension between agent autonomy and operational oversight.

CHAPTER 9: WHAT GOOD LOOKS LIKE

- **MIT / Harvard Medical School / eight additional institutions.** Agentic AI deployment for cancer immunotherapy adverse event surveillance, 2026. Full case study: less than 20% of effort on AI, over 80% on delivery discipline.

- **Starbucks / Deep Brew.** AI platform development timeline 2017-2026. Deep Brew project began 2017, platform launched 2019, expanded to inventory, staffing, store operations, real estate selection. Generative AI integrated 2024. Green Dot Assist (barista AI on Azure OpenAI) rolling out fiscal 2026. Industry analysts estimate 30% ROI. Rewards programme: 33.8 million active members by Q4 fiscal 2024.

- **Salesforce / Agentforce.** Early deployment failures in heavily customised enterprise environments. Agents skipped steps, business rules fired inconsistently, edge cases collided with legacy automation. Salesforce response: shift to metadata-first, deterministic guardrails, data-first design principle.

- **Deloitte.** State of AI in the Enterprise, 2026. 3,235 leaders, 24 countries. Leadership-driven governance correlated with significantly greater business value. Only one in five companies has a mature governance model. Number of companies with 40%+ AI in production expected to double within the year.

- **ETR (Enterprise Technology Research).** Tech Trends Feedback Panel, 2026. Enterprise IT leader quoted: "Once we put all those data points on it, the governance became much more fact-based than emotion based."

CHAPTER 10: THE ACCOUNTABILITY CONVERGENCE

- **Gartner.** 2025 AI Prediction Series. Fragmented AI regulation projected to quadruple by 2030, extending to 75% of the world's economies, driving over $1 billion in total compliance spend. "Death by AI" legal claims projected to exceed one thousand by end of 2026.

- **Colorado SB 205.** AI Act effective June 30, 2026. High-risk AI in employment, lending, insurance, legal services. Penalties: $20,000 per violation. NIST AI RMF / ISO 42001 compliance creates rebuttable presumption.

- **EU AI Act.** August 2, 2026 enforcement for high-risk AI systems. Penalties: up to 35 million euros or 7% of worldwide annual turnover.

- **Texas HB 149.** Responsible AI Governance Act, effective June 2025. AI for restricted decisions. Penalties: $10,000 to $200,000 per violation.

- **Illinois HB 3773.** Amended Illinois Human Rights Act, effective January 2024. Discriminatory AI in employment. Enforced through Illinois Human Rights Act procedures.

- **Australia.** Privacy Act reforms targeting automated decision-making, expected December 2026.

- **SEC.** Cybersecurity disclosure rules. First guidance issued 2011, Mandatory board-level cybersecurity disclosure rules arrived in July 2023, with compliance required by December 2023 for large companies and June 2024 for smaller reporting companies. Referenced as precedent for regulatory compression in AI governance.

- **IEEE.** Standard 3119-2025. Formal standard for procurement of AI and automated decision systems.

- **NIST.** AI Risk Management Framework. Four pillars: Govern, Map, Measure, Manage.

- **ISO 42001.** AI management system standard.

- **Australian Government.** AI Model Clauses, published March 2025.

- **Wilson Sonsini.** Late 2025 analysis noting that Colorado's legislative amendment did not change fundamental compliance requirements.

- **Cyber insurance market.** Early 2026 reports of insurers requiring AI Security Riders with mandatory disclosure of AI decision-making systems as a condition of policy renewal.

CHAPTER 11: WHERE YOU STAND

- **Deloitte.** State of AI in the Enterprise, 2026. Referenced for four out of five enterprises lacking mature governance for autonomous agents, and the doubling of production deployments.

CHAPTER 12: THE FIVE-AGENT TEST

- **Starbucks / Deep Brew.** Referenced for "began with one use case in 2017. The discipline came first. The scale came later."

KEY CONCEPTS

The following terms and frameworks are introduced or defined in this book. Page references correspond to the chapter where each concept is first established.

- **The Pilot Trap** The structural pattern where a successful AI pilot creates the confidence to deploy, but the delivery model that governed the pilot cannot sustain the system in production. The technology crosses the finish line. The organisation does not. (Chapter 1)

- **The Category Error** The misapplication of deterministic delivery models to probabilistic AI systems. Every management decision downstream, testing, governance, staffing, budgets, success metrics, inherits the mistake. The structural explanation for the 95% pilot failure rate. (Chapter 2)

- **The Thirty-Year Satisfying Assumption** The belief that a system tested is a system finished. It held for every technology that came before AI. It does not hold now. (Chapter 2)

- **The Demo God Curse** The better the pilot performs, the less prepared the organisation is for production. The demo creates the confidence. Production reveals the cost. (Chapter 3)

- **Negative Unit Economics** The inversion point where an AI agent costs more per task than the human process it replaced. A structural consequence of deploying probabilistic systems through financial governance designed for deterministic technology. (Chapters 3, 4)

- **Governance Theatre** The appearance of governance without the operational substance to detect, prevent, or respond to the failure modes that probabilistic systems produce. Worse than no governance, because it produces invisible degradation behind documentation that says everything is under control. (Chapter 3)

- **The 1:1 Planning Ratio** For every dollar approved to build an AI agent, at least one additional dollar will be required in the first twelve months of operations. For agents in regulated industries or high-volume production environments, the ratio is closer to two. (Chapter 4)

- **System Stewardship** The ongoing practice of monitoring, evaluating, governing, and adapting AI systems in production. Project management is an operating model for building things. System stewardship is an operating model for working alongside things that change. (Chapter 5)

- **The Five Control Surfaces** Business Alignment, Integration Architecture, Governance and Compliance, Observability and Evaluation, Orchestration and Operations. The minimum set of control dimensions required for an enterprise to claim it is managing its AI systems rather than merely running them. All five required simultaneously. (Chapter 6)

- **Agent Coaching** The continuous practice of evaluating, calibrating, and adjusting AI agent behaviour in production. Not a training programme. The operating expense of keeping a probabilistic system aligned with the business outcome it was deployed to serve. (Chapter 8)

- **The Coaching Loop** The agent acts. The system evaluates. The human decides. Every step is recorded. The loop is the discipline. A five-stage continuous cycle that maps to the five control surfaces. (Chapter 8)

- **The Production-Ready Threshold** The entry point to Scalable maturity. Enterprises below this threshold have identifiable gaps that create measurable risk in production AI operations. (Chapter 11)

- **The Five-Agent Test** A one-week diagnostic. Pick the five production AI agents that matter most. Conduct five conversations, one per control surface. Score a single-page scorecard. The findings reveal what has been invisible since deployment. (Chapter 12)

- **The AI Role Operating Framework™ (AI ROF™)** The operating model for how enterprises must restructure accountability, governance, and delivery when the technology they deploy is probabilistic. Encompasses five control surfaces, four leadership roles (the AI Architect, the AI Product Manager, the AI Delivery Manager, and the AgentOps Lead), and the system stewardship discipline that connects them. (Preface, Chapters 5, 6, 7).

ACKNOWLEDGEMENTS

The thesis in this book was confirmed by practitioners before it was published. CIOs, CAIOs, delivery leads, and programme directors across industries and geographies read early drafts, tested the arguments against their own experience, and told me where the diagnosis held and where it did not. Most of them cannot be named. The book is sharper because of what they shared.

The subscribers of The AI Delivery Discipline newsletter deserve a specific acknowledgement. Over two thousand senior leaders across industries and geographies contributed something no single research report could: a continuous signal from inside the enterprises where these patterns play out every day. Each issue surfaced data points, objections, and operational realities from practitioners who are living the pilot-to-production gap in real time. The category error thesis was not tested once and published. It was tested across every issue, refined by every response, and strengthened by every practitioner who told me what they were seeing on the ground. This book was written for them. It was also written with them.

Mark Cameron, CEO of Alyve and Forbes contributor, wrote the foreword. He also gave the most rigorous feedback the manuscript received. His challenge on the rational actor assumption, the observation that some leaders will resist the discipline because it threatens their authority, not because they disagree with the diagnosis, made the book more honest. His work alongside Vinod Bijlani, Sharma Madiraju, and me on the Intelligence-Centred Enterprise research series deepened the systems thinking that runs through every chapter. The AI Role Operating Framework predates the ICE collaboration, but the collaboration sharpened how I apply it.

Jim Berry, CEO of ADAPT, and the team at ADAPT saw the pattern before the book named it. Jim validated the thesis as an operating model mismatch, not a technology problem, and opened the door to the CxO community this book was written for. Anthony Saba, Managing Director of Transformation Services at ADAPT, brought conviction that the Australian enterprise market needs this discipline and gave the book its first distribution pathway.

Vinod Bijlani, AI Practice Leader for Asia-Pacific at HPE, read the manuscript and named the Five Control Surfaces framework as the operational core of the argument. That specificity, from someone who sees enterprise AI delivery at that scale, told me the framework had landed where it needed to land.

Mark Fay, Head of IT Management and Project Delivery at Westpac, reviewed the manuscript voluntarily and invited me to present the thesis to 170 practitioners inside one of Australia's largest banks. His willingness to put the argument in front of the people who would be accountable for implementing it was a test the book needed to pass.

Brandon Daniel designed and typeset both The AI Delivery Manager Blueprint and The Pilot Trap. His consistency across both books gave the body of work a visual identity that matches its intellectual ambition.

Meenatchi Ponnuraj, Business Analyst Manager, AETNA (CVS Health), read the manuscript with fresh eyes and no obligation to be kind. She told me where the argument lost her, where the language excluded her, and where the book assumed knowledge it had not yet earned. Every passage that survived her scrutiny is clearer because of it.

My wife Shantha, and my daughters Anika and Spoorthy, lived with this book for longer than anyone should have to. It was there in the early mornings before the house woke up, in the weekends I spent writing instead of being present, and in the evenings when I was physically at the table but mentally inside a chapter. They did not get the hours back. They did not get the attention back. What they gave me was the space to finish something I could not put down, and the grace to never once make me feel guilty for picking it up. This book exists because they let it.

ABOUT THE AUTHOR

Vijayan Seenisamy is an enterprise AI delivery strategist and the creator of the AI Role Operating Framework™ (AI ROF™), the model for how enterprises must restructure accountability when the technology they deploy is probabilistic.

Over twenty years he has led enterprise delivery programmes, technology delivery programmes, and digital transformations across manufacturing, retail, banking, telecom, insurance, media, and public sector. That work spanned consulting and enterprise roles at Accenture, Telstra, Deloitte, Bupa, and Woolworths Group, moving from production code to strategic delivery to operating model architecture.

His first book, The AI Delivery Manager Blueprint, defined the first of four leadership roles that enterprise AI delivery requires. The Pilot Trap defines the operating discipline those roles serve.

His research and frameworks on enterprise AI delivery reach over 10,000 senior leaders globally through LinkedIn, where his audience is concentrated among CIOs, CTOs, CAIOs, CFOs, CEOs and transformation leaders at enterprises with 10,000 or more employees. His biweekly newsletter, The AI Delivery Discipline, provides the diagnostic layer of his work to enterprise leaders building AI delivery capability.

He speaks on enterprise AI delivery at conferences and summits, advises enterprises on AI delivery maturity, and is a co-author of the Intelligence-Centred Enterprise research series.

He lives in Melbourne, Australia, with his wife and two daughters.

Connect: linkedin.com/in/vijayan-seenisamy

Newsletter: The AI Delivery Discipline